FAITH ᵀᴹ

VS.

THE **FORCE** OF	THE **POWER** OF
DESTRUCTION	CREATION

A personal look into real success and lasting peace through a unique analysis of two men

Wade Rich
Fear-less Innovations

Library of Congress Cataloging-in-Publication Data

Paperback ISBN: 978-1-4507-0232-4

2nd edition, October 2010

For more information on living fearlessly go to:
Live-Fearless.com

™

DEDICATION

TO MY CHILDREN

It is my joy that this is your starting point. May you know the only task you have here is to be happy. May you feel the freedom to let your light shine for the world. May you have the faith to see how truly beautiful it is.

TO MY WIFE

May you always see the beautiful savior that you are; the pure shining example of how powerful God truly is to have created you. I am forever blessed and changed by your pure and simple love. This book is the result of your love and faith in me. What an amazing creator you are.

TO MYSELF

May you forever see the "God" within yourself that you may have the power to see it in all mankind around you.

CONTENTS

PREFACE

This book is my story. Just like everyone else, I've ridden the roller coaster of life. This is my epiphany, my life changing story. It started when I was at rock-bottom, and I share the answers that have brought me out into a whole new world.

Growing up, I believed faith was somehow tied only to religion. I now realize I couldn't have understood it more backwards. Faith is the power of belief. And this book is specifically focused on faith outside of organized religion.

My previous misconception of faith and religion finally came to a head as my beliefs brought me to a place utter hopelessness. It took nearly losing it all to force me to face my fears and find real faith. A very personal and intimate part of this journey for me was my research into the lives of two men. I had a deep premonition that if I understood these two men better, somehow I'd understand myself better. And I did.

This new paradigm has been an answer to nearly every problem I've struggled with in my life. It is my sincere pleasure to share what has brought me to a place of peace I didn't realize was possible, in the hope that reading about my shift might bring a source of joy into your life as well.

Sincerely,

CHAPTER 1

™

FEAR ECLIPSE

It was January 2007. The room was completely dark except the sliver of light shining through the crack under the door. I lay on my bed, tortured nearly out of my mind. I was at the bottom—again. My wife and three children were somewhere else, too scared of the current state of mind I was in to be anywhere near me.

"This world would be better off without you! Your family would be better off without you! The businesses would be better off without you," I told myself.

"Where are you, God? Now that I'm at my lowest point?! I've always been there for you! I served you as a missionary, testifying to others about you. About how great and loving and kind you are. About how you'll never let them down. I pay regular tithes to the church. I've spent hours away from my family every week performing church duties. I've been a teacher and leader in the church for more than 14 years. I keep the commandments, read my scriptures, and do everything I'm supposed to.

So where are you now—now that I'm in the pit of despair, the darkest abyss? Where have you always been when I lose hope? Why can't you lift me up? Why can't you perform some miracle? Can't you see I'm losing it?! Can't you be there when I'm down—or am I just too bad right now? Have I fallen out of your graces? Maybe I never had your grace to begin with! Maybe you don't even exist and I've been talking to myself all these years. Maybe it's all just a big joke, and I'm the butt of it!"

"Oh, quit making excuses, Wade. Just be a man and give everyone else around you a break. You're a failure; you've always been a failure. Think of all the people you've

conned into believing in you. Think of everyone you're dragging down. Do you want to keep taking advantage of them by going on with your life? Please do them all a favor—if you really care about them, give up. Or if you're a spineless loser, feel free to keep dragging them along while you live this pathetic joke of a life. At least you're smart enough to know how you could do it right now, right here in this room. It would be simple and quick, and you'd at least leave this world having performed one brave act."

Holy crap! I had allowed myself to ride this train many times in the past, but never had it gone this far. And the conductor just announced the next stop was the last one. Never before had I given so much belief to my fears, never before had I given them so much power. I realized at that moment I had only two choices—either I give in to the darkness suffocating me, or I get up and walk away. I instinctively knew it was black and white; it was one or the other.

I decided I would give it one more chance. I knew my fate if I stayed in that room. And I knew I could always come back if it didn't work. But I'd give my life this one last try.

I was scared—scared to my core. For the first time in my life, I was very seriously thinking about ending it. I was so low—not even the thought of my three beautiful, precious children and my precious wife could sway me in the least. And that realization scared me the most. Somehow, after what felt like an eternity, I began to fight. I now knew I had to get out of that room, but this monster was stronger than any force I'd ever felt.

It laid on my soul, paralyzing me. It took EVERYTHING I had to roll off that bed. My feet felt like they weighed a ton. Despite this darkness, somehow I knew, if I just walked out of the bedroom, something would happen. It had to, or I was truly lost. Even though the other side of me had no faith whatsoever and fought me every step of the way.

I trudged to the door and opened it as the darkness in my soul screamed, *"NO! Don't do it, you LOSER! Don't torture your family one more minute with your miserable existence!"* Every step I took down the hallway was exhausting. *"Yeah, good one, let's go spread the darkness to your wife—that's just what she needs,"* the voice mocked.

I finally reached the family room where my wife sat alone, the children in bed now. I painfully made my way to the couch and sat down, my eyes swollen and bloodshot from crying, my head pounding from the emotional pressure and stress. I was out of faith. I had no belief that anything could be done to help or save me. I just sat, oozing negative energy. My wife, although scared by my hurtful behavior a few hours earlier, stared at me, not sure what to say at first. But then, miraculously, she was inspired to say exactly what I needed to hear.

She looked me in the eye with an undeniable conviction. *"Wade, you are NOT alone. God and your dad are with you right in this moment, weeping with you."*

The darkness in me wanted to laugh but couldn't, because the second she said it, I knew it was true. I could feel it like a shaft of light splitting the darkness. She went on patiently for the next hour to refute all of the lies I had let build up in my mind.

She told me I was NOT a failure, but a completely successful husband and wonderful father. And, little by little, she shed light on the darkness in my mind, forcing it to flee, quenching my fears. I was amazed she made it through the wall I built up. I don't remember ever being more scared. But suffice it to say, climbing out of such mental and spiritual anguish was a lifesaving miracle—and, most of all, a MAJOR turning point.

What really made the difference was my wife's love and faith. My greatest fear at that point was that I was separated from God. I felt I had tallied up the good and bad in my life and reached the dreadful conclusion—I was BAD, worthless, a loser. And my conclusion felt final. When you're inherently "bad," there's only one "good" thing you can do—get rid of the "bad." I was the trash God would eventually have to throw out anyway. And truth be told, it wasn't just myself I had to think was bad; I had to think God was messed up as well. After all, it was He who had created me in the first place, right?

When my wife spoke to me, her love was so pure and sweet, her faith so strong, I had to acknowledge a major contradiction in my mind. If God created my wife and she could be this unconditionally loving and kind, how could He NOT be AT LEAST as loving and kind as she was? I was beginning to recognize that maybe the problem was in my mind. Maybe it wasn't me, and maybe it wasn't God. Maybe it was my *beliefs*. I didn't understand it all, but I knew I could not deny the purity, truth and power of her love.

I'd had several similar experiences to this one previously, but this was the final straw. Despite all the "good" things I was doing in my life, I had a major problem. Every six months or so, negativity would pile up on me, and I'd find myself drowning in depression and despair. I was struggling every day to be happy, a perfectionist who wasn't satisfied, even when I accomplished a goal. Each time I rode this fear train, it was harder and harder to get off. And next time, I'd probably end up riding it all the way to its one-way destination.

I was now forced to look at the problem, which I already knew was in my head—I just wasn't sure where. I knew one fact: I didn't *need* anything else to be happy. I had every essential ingredient for happiness. I had a wonderful marriage; my love for my wife is unfathomable to me. I had three absolutely wonderful children I adored. I was blessed financially to have all of my needs covered.

I was further blessed to work with my two brothers and best friends. I was even blessed with the opportunity to manage my father's business, which meant I was my own boss. I'd always been blessed with good health—and the list goes on.

So why was I so unhappy? I wasn't visibly depressed and down every day. In fact, most people around me would characterize me as a positive and happy person. Happiness, however, was something I would display, but it never seemed to reach the core of my heart. It was as though happiness was warmth that came from the outside, but I recognized the center was still cold. When that outside warmth wasn't there, it couldn't provide its own heat as I somehow knew it should.

What I eventually came to realize was that my ability to be happy there all along—it was just blurred by a layer of fear that kept me from really being able to bask in it. This fear was based on a load of false beliefs I'd picked up through life, some from my parents, some from my misinterpreted religious beliefs, and others from various people and experiences. These false beliefs were running 24/7 in the back of my mind, causing static and feedback that was blocking me from peace and joy. They were also the number one source of every bit of negativity in my life. They were fear-spawning and I came to realize I was afraid of nearly everything!

And the more I thought about it, the more I realized the real problem was fear. In every instance where I was robbed of happiness and peace, fear was always the culprit.

Realizing these fears could eventually destroy my life, very literally, I determined that I had to learn how to understand and manage them. Since that day I've stumbled onto a gold mine of light and knowledge that has changed every area of my life.

Back at that time something my older brother said really cemented my determination. *"You know, whether there's a Higher Power that loves and cares about us or not, really doesn't matter. I'd rather live a happy life believing there is than live a miserable life fearing there isn't, because whether there is or isn't, the power to be happy is in our hands. Faith really IS the key."*

As I looked back, I was stunned by how much time and energy I wasted being AFRAID! And being afraid of what? Afraid of failure, afraid of success, afraid of not making money, afraid of making money, afraid of not being a good son, husband, father, friend—you name it, I was afraid of it! What a waste of time! And the real clincher is, none of it was even real.

Let's just suppose, for argument's sake, there really isn't a higher power, but everyone believes and acts as if there *is* a higher power. Don't we get the exact same results? It's like Santa Claus; whether he exists or not doesn't matter. If my children believe he does, they still get the benefits of that belief. You can picture the feelings of excitement and hope they feel based on their belief in him, and then their faith is fulfilled through the gifts they receive. I mean, my kids hope for things that when I hear about it from my wife, my first reaction is, "Oh Hell No! We can NOT afford that." But you KNOW what happens; I don't even have to say it. They get it—somehow they get it! And what did they have to do to get it!? Believe! That's it!

My point is not to prove a Higher Power doesn't exist. My point is even if He does exist, it doesn't matter if we don't believe it. So technically, it doesn't matter if God exists or not—what matters is what you believe, because in your BELIEF is where the power lies.

My newfound determination is to live in faith for faith's sake, and nothing else. This means I uproot fear as much as possible out of my life, because the principle works the same in reverse. If you fear something, it doesn't matter whether it exists or not, you still get the same results.

For example, we've all had the experience of lying in bed at night and hearing a sound. Your fearful imagination takes off and before long you've played out this whole horrible scene in your mind. You finally get the courage to check things out and sure enough the monster you'd envisioned was not there to destroy you and your loved ones. But yet you felt all the feelings you would have felt if someone really had broken in. So whether someone broke in or not didn't matter—you still got the same results.

Now you may say, "But what if someone REALLY does break in, and my worst nightmare came true and they hurt me and my family?" My answer would still be, your fear in the midst of that crisis would only consummate the negativity of it. What I mean by that is eventually you'll see that fear at one point or another was at the source of that break-in to begin with. You then would be feeling the results of that negative energy. Your fear then only adds to the bonfire of negativity multiplying it that much more. Fear is worthless. To be even more accurate it's of less value than worthless (assuming that by worthless we are giving it a value based on a positive scale of zero or very close to zero). As far as value goes fear is negative on the scale. When something happens which has an inherent negative source of energy your fear actually validates and supports that negativity. Conversely if you respond to a scary situation in faith you'll be able to think clearly and act based on truth.

We live in a time when fear is predominant—with natural disasters increasing worldwide, terrorist attacks hitting home in our own country, and random shootings and killings seemingly everywhere. Political lines have become more pronounced between liberals and conservatives, and our country is sinking into fear. We need to realize that none of what you fear actually exists—at least not yet. You see, faith and fear are actually dealing with one common thing—the unknown. Faith deals with the unknown with optimism, hope, and positive belief. Fear deals with the unknown with negativity, hopelessness, and despair. I've learned how to minimize and even eliminate the power of fear in my life and through knowledge you can as well.

I firmly believe there are two forces that govern our universe—one positive, the other negative. And the controlling factor for these powers lies within us—one is faith and the other fear. Faith the power of creation, fear is the force of destruction.

CHAPTER 2

TM

HOW WILL THIS BOOK BENEFIT ME?

The first fear about a book like this is that it's going to tell you what's wrong with you. This couldn't be further from the truth. I've spent all my life fearing what is wrong with me. Now I realize I've missed the whole point. Instead of asking what's wrong with me, I now ask what's right with me. That's my goal here. To tell you what's RIGHT with you, what's RIGHT with everyone else, and to help you see you don't actually have any problems or obstacles—at least not real ones that stand in the way of your happiness. I'll help you see that happiness and peace are much, much closer than you may now realize.

My purpose is not to change anyone. I believe all people are good-natured or, thus, "God- natured". I don't believe there is any reason to change "who" a person is. Since good, or God, is at the core of each of us, it simply needs to be recognized, uncovered, and accepted.

I believe the source of good in each of us, which I call our heart of gold, is like a bottomless reservoir of the finest, purest metal alloy. It emerges from the reservoir clean and pure and is then energized by our foundational beliefs. Based on the energy level of these beliefs, this metal leaves the factory with either a positive or negative charge, resulting in our actions.

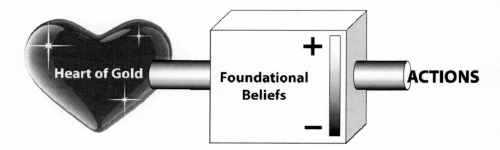

It's important to understand this paradigm or viewpoint now because the key to opening our heart to new information is feeling secure. As human beings, we tend to guard our hearts like hawks. Only in situations where we don't fear attack do we open and allow new information in.

The importance of this "heart-of-gold" paradigm is it shows that negative energy doesn't come from a person's core, but from their foundational beliefs which charge the good source with a negative charge. This empowers us to understand and function more positively with others. Most of all, it helps us be more open to new information, without the fear of being attacked or having our core fears validated.

The other value of this paradigm is to understand changing negative actions can be as simple as changing the underlying negative beliefs. There's no reason to change the person themselves—only the belief!

In this book, I'll be sharing my experiences and understanding of the negative foundational beliefs that kept me hostage to fear and how I replaced those with true, positive beliefs. I'll offer the tools and techniques I've learned to use to help discern the forces that are driving my actions, whether they be faith or fear.

It's common to fear people out there who are just itching to tell us there is something wrong with us and we need to change. This gets interpreted as, "you are bad" or, "there is a bad part of you that needs to be changed." Guilt and fear are the ultimate tools of negativity that cannot be used for good. A tool of negativity can ONLY bring more negative results. It cannot and will not bring about positive energy or results.

A WORLD IN FEAR

Fear seems to be the language everyone speaks and we all understand. Just turn on the evening news. Fear is a learned response, unknowingly passed on to keep us vigilant and "safe." Fear is ever-present in every level of society— marketing, communication, media, and relationships. Its prevalence and predominance has a costly impact on us financially and emotionally.

Current statistics show depression affects more people than almost any other single disease. Depression is also a major factor in many other diseases. More than 20% of Americans are seeking professional help for depression, and this doesn't account for the countless others who are suffering silently.

What is depression? To put it simply, it's a lack of peace and happiness. It's a low spot, a void of hope, and joy. What causes depression? There are a lot of different answers; some point to physiological causes like chemical imbalances. I believe fear is the root cause of all depression.

As I've studied, I found case after case of individuals describing the cause of their depression as fear. After the attack on September 11, 2001, many stories were written about the emotional effects the attack had on our country. It exposed the fear of millions of Americans. Reports show people from all parts of the country were seriously impacted as more individuals sought professional help than at any other time.

In my research, I came across an individual who suffered from Post Traumatic Stress Disorder (PTSD). Below is a quote from [1]John R. as to what he believes the cause to be.

"I wanted to write about my thoughts concerning my PTSD, it's effects and what I feel might be helpful to other suffers and their families. I'm not a doctor or scientist. In fact, what I share here might be completely unscientific. FEAR!

While doing some research about my PTSD, I've run across lists of symptoms that I suffer from. I've done a great deal of soul searching in an attempt to get to the root emotions. For example, anger is a major symptom for me, but I started to wonder if anger was the root emotion, or is it a secondary emotion. As I continued down the list of symptoms, I started to notice a common root factor behind every symptom listed. Fear appears to be the root emotion behind every symptom that I have."

Fear is the root cause of depression or lack of peace and happiness. This life is about overcoming our fears and finding peace. This book isn't about finding the problems—it's about seeing the solutions.

You'll learn there is no such thing as a "bad" person. The only issue to even address is the fact we all get the results of the energy we choose to work with—positive or negative—faith or fear.

My purpose is to help you see your true positive worth and confirm that

---

[1] John R. Post Traumatic Stress Disorder Forum – www.ptsdforum.org/threads/5790-fear-root-cause

you are of infinite worth as a positive, faithful being. Not only are you worthy of love, you are loved—and you ARE love. You are inseparably connected to love because love is what you ARE. It's who you truly are—faithful, positive, pure… love.

My hope is that this book will bear the positive fruits of hope, peace, joy, enthusiasm, and allow the love inside you to flow freely.

CHAPTER 3

FAITH: THE KEY TO PROGRESSION

The universal message of this book is outside the lines of race, country and, most of all, religion. We hear the word faith, and immediately attach it to religion. I want to introduce the concept of faith to you in the most universal sense, without the attachments of religious persuasion. Accordingly, I hope to communicate this message in a way any individual can understand and take the truths they find and be uplifted, whether Atheist, Jewish, Christian, Muslim, or just plain confused (which I think has encompassed all of us at one point in our lives).

These universal principles apply to EVERYONE. In order for you to be able to accept anything that might be positive from this book, please understand you'll have to open your mind and let go of any fears that prevent you from learning and growing. If nothing else, let this be your first exercise of faith, allowing yourself to be open to information that could be useful to you. We've all heard the statement, "Knowledge is Power". It's true! Anytime you open yourself to more learning outside of what you already know, you've gained more knowledge, which is more power.

I used to be stuck in "the fear of learning" box. I had my religion, my core beliefs, and I felt it was the one and only source of truth for me. However, I allowed myself to draw other unwarranted conclusions, such as, *because this is the one and only source of truth for me, any information from an outside source, is no good.*

OUCH! Looking back now, anyone could see how foolish and damning (meaning the literal stopping of learning and growth) this belief is. It was the fear of others, the fear that everyone else was going the wrong way, so I'd better not pay any attention to them or I would be led astray as well. And even deeper than that, it was a fear of God, or at least confusion about God. Think about this for a second: if we've all divided ourselves into different religions, we obviously think whatever we believe at the moment is correct. So what does that make what everyone else believes? To some extent, we must believe that they are wrong. And regardless of whether they are right, we are right, or neither is right, it only makes sense that we are more likely to find truth if we look everywhere instead of just inside our own boxes.

When I realized I was overlooking a vast amount of information by sentencing myself to my own little informational jail cell, I began to see my own faith in a whole new light. And now I see a whole new world where I am free to find truth from any source! Before, I was stuck eating the same informational diet over and over; now I've moved to a banquet table that is the world, laden with every type of informational food I could imagine! Whether it be the Bible, a science journal, Winston Churchill, Gandhi, or my child; truth can be found everywhere: from a religious expert to a rock star! I've stopped judging the source and started judging the information.

My purpose in this book is to help you increase faith in yourself and in your fellow man. Therefore, the ultimate goal of this book is unity. It has been said that eventually religion and science will meet. I believe that means science, the physical or factual search of truth, and religion, the spiritual search for truth, eventually will both find the same answers. And I believe we are all searching for those same answers. Just as 1 + 1 = 2, no matter what race or religion you are, there are powers upon which our universe is governed, the powers of faith and fear.

Faith is the force that propels us as human beings. Whether you recognize it or not, we all have faith in something. For example, right now you must have some amount of faith you'll get something out of reading this book, otherwise you wouldn't be reading it.

But the Faith I'm talking about is NOT ignorance meaning based upon foolishness or falsehood. Just the contrary, real faith is actually the power to act based on truth. All the best things in life are obtained through acts of faith Long term relationships, children, following your heart; all of these things are difficult since they require us to overcome fear. But, we do them because we believe the truth that happiness will come from it. Even business decisions that are completely logical steps, take faith. Investing even when we have all the facts and figures in front of us still is not always easy. It may be very clear cut logical decision—to make a return on an investment, we have to invest first. But fear is always there to cloud the truth and make even the simplest of decisions difficult.

Fear is the ultimate damnation. I mean that in its very literal sense. Fear does one thing and does it perfectly—stops our progression. It cuts us off from learning and growth like nothing else can. Just as faith creates action, fear paralyzes. You remember as kids if something scared you, like the monster under the bed, you'd be FROZEN with fear! The fear of failure is the number one reason for lack of action. I have a statement written on the wall above my computer screen that reads, "*What would you do if you knew you couldn't fail?*"

As I've talked about Fear vs. Faith with others outside my inner circle, the first argument I get from skeptics is, "*Well, you can't really believe all fear is negative, right?*" Then they do their best to think of extreme example how fear can actually save you. For example, if you're on the battle field, doesn't fear give you the power and motivation to help you stay alive? I tell them it's a great question and then clarify that, based on fear the way I define it, the answer is no.

FEAR AND THE BRAIN

There was an incredible documentary done by the *History Channel* called, *The Brain*. One segment specifically targeted the emotion of fear and how it works in the brain.

The brain is built of layers; the amygdala is in the lowest or "oldest" layer in the brain. It controls the unconscious functions, such as breathing, heart rate, emotional responses and hormone secretions. Most of all, it controls the autonomic responses associated with fear.

The highest or "newest" layer of the brain is the frontal cortex. This is the part of our brain that makes us human. It is the conductor of the brain, synchronizing all the other parts. This is where we use knowledge to make clear calculated decisions.

Scientists have recently found that, when our senses detect fear, the amygdala is the first to receive the message. It takes twice as long for the frontal cortex to receive the message. Because our frontal cortex has not yet had the chance to work through the problem logically, we instinctively want to respond in one of three ways: fight, flight or freeze.

The amygdala begins pumping adrenaline and cortisol hormones into the blood stream. Heart rate and breathing increase, and you're now surging with all kinds of energy and pain tolerance. But until the frontal cortex has a chance to work out the correct response, you won't know how to act to use this power properly. In many cases the amygdala begins the "freak-out" process for something that isn't even real; for example, hearing that "bump" in the dark.

Now if fight, flight or freeze happens to be the right response before the frontal cortex can produce the correct response, it's simply coincidence. In most cases it will NOT be the desired response. It is the fear of the unknown that causes us not to know how to react, because until the frontal cortex gets more information, it's in the dark and you're left to the mercy of your amygdala, which is sending the "freak-out" alert.

The philosophy of the Navy Seals is an incredible example of how fear affects us and our actions. Roger Herbert, Commanding Officer, Navy Seals, lays the foundation by stating, *"When you look at historic mistakes on the battle field, they're almost always associated with fear or with panic, so the capacity to control these impulses is extremely important."*

The Navy Seals training is carefully calculated to achieve one goal—to retrain the brain to override the amygdala's fear / panic response and go to the frontal cortex for problem solving. The way they do this is very intense. The recruits are submerged in a world of stress and chaos from day one. They're exposed to exercises such as the Hooded Box Drill where the student's head is covered in a black hood. They are blind and deaf until suddenly the hood is yanked off and they are presented with a situation. Each situation is different. One situation could be an opponent attacking them viciously and violently. Another could be someone else being attacked. The next situation could be someone kindly asking which way to the next gas station.

In these extremes we see how important overriding the natural urge to respond in fear truly is. One situation requires lethal action, where the other requires a simple helping hand. Through this exercise they're trained NOT to react in fear, but to use knowledge and facts to decide on an appropriate response.

The most infamous Brain Training exercise is the Underwater Pool Competency Test. Here students must face what's called a super fear...the fear of drowning. Prior to the test they're trained how to deal with each of the scenarios they will have to face and are drilled over and over on how to resolve them. Then they're fitted with scuba gear and placed into the pool. Once under water, they are subjected to controlled and planned harassment. Instructors attack students and remove their oxygen source. They tie the oxygen tubes into knots, shut off the oxygen flow etc. The student must then calmly override their natural fear-panic response and solve the problems with their oxygen source, if they panic and surface for air, they fail the test. More students fail this test than any other.

One student interviewed stated how scary it was standing in line waiting to be next and watching your comrades being tested. Seeing others fail fueled the fears of, "If he couldn't pass it, will I be able to?"

It's a perfect example why reacting to fearful situations in fear is not productive. It doesn't mean we won't feel scared, but it means that, despite the fear, we turn to our source of knowledge and faith for the desired response to produce a positive result.

FAITHFUL PROGRESSION

Think of things you feel truly inspired to do in your life, but fear prevents you from doing them. What gives you the power to overcome your fear? The only missing ingredient is faith. Now I know this may seem like an over-simplification. You may have convinced yourself you can't due to a lack of money, physical limitations, or some other limiting belief. I assure you these become nothing more than excuses for your fear. I can say this because I've pursued a lot of different inspirations in my life and passed up many. Know that there is one and only one force that powers accomplishment. Faith is the fuel that drives positive movement in life. Everything else is just details. Faith is the key.

What is Faith *really?* It's a positive belief that produces action. It can be an action as simple as turning on a light switch. You believe if you flip the switch, the light will come on. Without faith, combined with knowledge, you'd most likely never flip the switch and not receive the blessing of light. With that in mind, let's talk about your level of faith, or as I like to call it, your circle of faith. Everyone has a circle of faith that includes the things they have enough faith to act upon.

Most everyone has flipping a light switch well within their circle of faith. What about things outside of that circle, such as losing a loved one, being hurt by another individual, or experiencing some other major tragedy?

It could also be something simple like wanting to learn how to dance, or to learn another language, or starting your own business. These are things that if you can't act upon right now or deal with from a place of peace and faith—then they're outside your circle of faith. The great news is your circle of faith can grow. This is the purpose of these types of events, to stretch our circle of faith until it can include those things.

Let's talk about the mechanics of this for a moment. We have faith that when we flip the light switch the light will come on. But what happens when we flip the switch and the light doesn't come on? For a small child who's never had this experience, it becomes an event outside his or her circle of faith. They could become confused and frustrated. But this is not outside an adult's circle because they understand most likely the bulb is burnt out and simply needs to be changed.

But what happens if the adult replaces the light bulb, and the light still doesn't work? This could be outside the adult's circle of knowledge and faith. This could even result in a fear such as, "What if the wiring is shorting out, and could start a fire?" Luckily, in most cases, we know to call someone, such as an electrician, who has a greater circle of faith and knowledge , to come resolve the problem.

Picture the circle of faith like a spotlight shining down on your life; the void outside that circle is ignorance, darkness and fear. Keep in mind, fear is not bad, or, in other words, we aren't bad because we fear. Fear is simply the opposite of faith.

The purpose of life is to stretch that circle of light. For example, until you've had a close loved one die, death remains outside your circle. Once it happens, if faith is applied, eventually that area becomes lit. If dealt with through faith, we can actually come to a place of peace and understanding in the face of something that initially seems so scary. Some things may stay outside your circle all of your life, such as your own death. Our current circle of light can help us have faith for the dark areas not currently lit.

Our intention is to learn how to more quickly and easily stretch your circle of faith. If something stays too long outside that circle, it will eventually start to consume your circle in reverse, destroying the faith you had in other things. And the nothingness outside your circle, being fear, can begin to envelop your faith.

I watched a documentary about the 9/11 tragedy of the Twin Towers in New York entitled *Where was God during 9/11?* The show interviewed the surviving spouses and families impacted by the disaster. Wives who used to "believe in God" were saying they just weren't sure anymore. Consequently, they weren't sure of anything in their life anymore! They were questioning everything. The bottom line is, they were consumed by fear. Faith is the foundation of life, and when it's gone, everything else begins to go with it.

Regardless of whether we acknowledge it or not, we are beings of power. Our power is the power to create. And all creation begins in the world of our mind, heart or soul. Religiously speaking, this could be called the spirit world.

Scientifically it would be called the fourth dimension. Despite its name, we can agree this is where all creation begins. Everything man has created had its birth in the womb of the mind and soul.

We ALL hold this power of creation. We don't get to choose whether or not we are creators—we just are. You can't say, "I'd like to forfeit my power. I don't want to create or affect things." Everything we think or believe is the act of wielding the creative power.

Faith and fear are the definitions of the type of creative energy we wield. Both are the same thing, the power of belief. One is based in the world of truth and light; the other in the world of darkness and illusion. We don't get the option whether or not we create. We only get the choice of what energy we use to create. In fact, you're doing it right now. You have thoughts in your mind right now that are creating a result in your life.

Faith and fear are the same thing—belief. Fear is actually faith. The only difference is that fear is faith going in the wrong direction.

So as an exercise of faith, I encourage you to open your mind and heart to the reception of truth. Your heart is the ultimate tool of truth recognition, if you let it be. Trust your heart never to let you down. Drop the wall of fear and let your heart tell you what is and isn't true. It's the walls of fear that keep your heart in ignorance and darkness.

One of the greatest steps of faith is to trust yourself.

CHAPTER 4

IS IT ALL BLACK OR WHITE?

We all have a tendency to judge things as black or white, right or wrong, good or bad. We have two buckets: one black, the other white. This system seems great. As we come across new things we have yet to classify, we quickly make a judgment based on whatever information we have at the time, and then sentence that belief, thing or even person to confinement in either one or the other—black or white—good or bad. It's true isn't it?

I've spent most of my life becoming the foremost expert on black and white classification. Many people I know are working towards the same. We believe if we get everything correct—if we get all of the bad things in the black bucket and the truly good things in the white bucket—then we've done it! Our lives are now a success because we've successfully classified everything properly. We securely hold onto the "good" things, and strictly abhor the "bad" ones. So what does that make us? If we know the difference between good and bad, but we choose the good so that makes us good—right?

The logic seems simple enough, and it's no wonder we come to that conclusion. When you look at how we parent our children, it's not hard to notice how we train the new generation. We use statements such as, "Eat your vegetables, they're GOOD for you." And, "Don't eat that, it's BAD for you." "Do this, because it's GOOD." "Don't do that, it's BAD." And most of all, "He's a GOOD guy" or, "He's a BAD guy." Most games children play and entertainment we watch is centered on good vs. evil, cops vs. robbers, cowboys vs. Indians, villains vs. heroes. The first aspect we look for in a story is to determine: who's the good guy and who's the bad guy.

I was playing a war-based video game with my son when he asked, *"Why'd you shoot him, Daddy?"* My unconscious answer was, *"Because he's a bad guy."*

Why do we form this black and white thinking, and how does it affect us? Everyone I've ever known has one thing in common: an inherent fear I call the core fear. I call it the core fear because all other fears are attached in some way to this central one. The core fear, simply put, is the fear of one's self. I stated earlier there is no reason to change who a person is. However, there is one change that can make all the difference, a change of perspective, going from a natural state of fear to a state of faith.

What is it that we fear about ourselves? We fear our hearts (as a reference to our true selves) to be black instead of white. We fear being bad, worthless, a failure, meaningless, and every other negative connotation. We fear being unworthy of heaven and deserving of hell. And because we fear being bad, it can become a desperate effort to classify good and bad as quickly as possible in order to determine our own worth, black or white.

It's how we struggle to find worth and security. We want desperately to understand everything around us. We want to find what is good, and do it. This will make us a good person, right? Here's the fate of the black and white mentality: at some point, you have to come to the realization that you're at least partly black, or thus partly bad. This triggers more frantic efforts towards goodness, and becomes a game only God knows the score of. You work to do and be "good enough" to out-weigh the bad you just can't seem to stop from coming out of you. Now it's just a fear-filled waiting game you don't get to see the score for until after you die.

And so throughout our life, we ride the black and white, up and down, nauseating roller coaster of fear. We're good one day and bad the next. And trust me, I've been in the front car, and I can ride it with the best, hands in the air screaming for my life. Again this roller coaster is, in my belief, the number one reason for the depression that's strangling our world.

I'd like to re-illustrate this principle in the most common universally accepted spiritual terms. Let's say there is a God, and a Devil. The comical example of an angel on our right shoulder and a Devil on the left sometimes feels all too real. So, looking at it in these terms, you have the Devil telling you you're his. Because being bad means you're like him, right? You also have your heart telling you it's not true. You can almost feel the tug-of-war between heaven and hell going on at times in your life.

Here's what I've found to be true. This system of black and white, good and bad, isn't real. It's nothing more than an illusion created by fear. There is no war between God and the Devil, each of them claiming, "He or she is mine!"

The reality is, **we are God's, period**. We are **not** the Devil's, and never will be. No more, than one of my children can be someone else's child. We are the creation of God, and nothing can change that fact. All the Devil has to work with is illusions. It's been that way since the beginning. You never were, nor ever will be lost, except in the illusion of fear. And the beauty is—the way out is simple and easy. The simple recognition of truth and reality, and the illusion falls away. No matter how much fear tells us we are lost. Our heart tells us we are NOT.

And that's the truth. You are not lost. You are God's. There is no fight. The only fight that occurs is in the illusionary world of fear. The Devil has no real power, except the illusionary power of lies. Thus, his greatest tool is fear. And our defense against it is faith.

The only black and white there is, is truth or deception. Our key to building faith is finding truth and deception, knowing the difference, and living accordingly.

Because of fear, we waste time trying to prove who we are to ourselves and everyone around us, and even if unconsciously, to God as well. The reality I hope to show you is we don't have to prove anything to our Creator. He knows who you are—because He created you.

I believe if God could say anything to us, it would be, *"Stop trying to PROVE who you are. And enjoy BEING who you are. I know you better than you know yourself. You are my son or daughter, and I know your worth. And it is priceless."* Most of all, His message to us always has and always will be—you are okay, period. Right here and right now, you're safe and you have nothing to fear.

There's a scripture, I just can't resist throwing in here. It used to have little positive effect on me until I read it through the eyes of faith. It's found in Luke 13:34 and reads, *"O Jerusalem, Jerusalem, thou that killest the prophets, and stonest them which are sent unto thee, how often would I have gathered thy children together, even as a hen gathereth her chickens under her wings, and ye would not!"*

Like with many scriptures it's easy, or should I say "natural," at first to assume negativity in this passage. It could sound, at first, like more condemnation. *"I tried to help you and save you from your 'bad' selves but you were just too bad!"* However, I see this completely opposite. I feel the Lord is saying, *"How many times when you were afraid, I've tried to comfort you. I tried to tell you it was okay, YOU were okay. I even sent men with a message of good news to relieve your fears, but you were so scared, like a rabid dog you bit the hand feeding you. I wasn't coming to validate the fears about yourself. Most of all I wasn't coming to tell you you're bad. You were the ones believing you're bad. I'm trying to communicate the reality that you are, and always will be, good!"*

And then my favorite line (in my own words) is, *"Oh how I want to gather you under my wings like a mother hen gathering her chicks, so you'll feel the comforting truth that you are okay. That you can feel your worth and value communicated through my fearless love for you. That you may feel the reality that nothing can hurt you. However, your fear makes you even afraid of me. Oh how I wish to impress upon you the reality that I AM your Savior, your protector, and you have nothing to fear."*

There's no fear in that statement whatsoever. He has nothing to fear because He knows we're okay, regardless of what happens. We're in His hands and there's no possible way of being taken away or jumping out. The statement is simply made in the hope we'll accept more peace and hope by letting our fears go.

Another fear you could have of this scripture, is He's implying there's a clock ticking. He WAS going to gather us and comfort us but hey, we've said no one too many times. And now He's just going to let the Devil have us.

We again must combat fear with faith. Which says; there is no end to His love and protection, just as there is no end to our value and worth. He has absolutely no fear for us, because we are in His hands. And so, despite this simple statement of ultimate peace, if we cannot see it through the eyes of faith, our desperately needed peace and happiness is blocked by our fears and its illusions.

Going back to the black and white mentality—if everything isn't black or white, good or bad, then what is it? I was raised with a very strong black and white mentality. And even as a teenager I knew clearly what was bad and what was good, and tried as hard as I could to avoid the bad. This created conflict within me, because some of these things I believed were bad, made me feel good. For example, I'd see movies made by "worldly men" or according to my belief system "bad men", but the messages contained in their work made me feel good.

I also struggled because I felt a love for all types of music, including rock music, which was straight from the Devil's hand, as far as I knew at the time. When I'd wonder why I liked a bad thing so much, I was told it was because the Devil is so good at making bad things feel good. At this point I was really confused because if I can't tell the difference between something that's good or bad, based on how it makes me feel, then I'm completely lost.

It's like if I eat something that's not good for me, I get the natural consequences of feeling bad. If I eat something that's good for me, I receive the consequences of feeling good. Why would spiritual things be any different? Accepting this mindset of judgment based on what people told me, was completely crazy. I was like a feather in the wind, blown and tossed by the fears of everyone around me.

Seeing things as bad confused me about God. How could God create bad things? Is He good or bad? Which is it? Through the eyes of faith you'll come to realize, as I did, it's not about good or bad, it's about learning and growth. The world isn't black and white; it's the whole spectrum of beautiful, glorious colors! Black and white thinking produces judgment, many times without all the facts. Only God Himself can know the full story. In the meantime, we should recognize and enjoy the full spectrum of vibrant colors we are surrounded by!

THE PARABLE OF THE FRUIT TREES

Judgment damns our progression and learning, as these two fruit farmers demonstrate.

There were once two neighboring fruit farmers who competed for the fruit market in their town. Both farmed similar-sized parcels of land. The farmer to the east prided himself on how quickly he could harvest the crop. Each harvest, he went down the rows, assessing the fruit of each tree. He could quickly tell by look and feel if the fruit was sweet or bitter.

He marked the trees producing sweet fruit for harvest, and to keep for another year. He marked the trees producing bitter fruit for burning and replanting. He went swiftly about his job, assessing the trees, keep… burn… keep… burn… burn… keep. Soon he was done, more quickly than his neighbor, and was the first to the market for selling his goods.

The farmer on the west, harvested differently. Much like his neighbor, he surveyed each tree to determine its fruit. He marked the trees producing sweet fruit for harvest. However, if the fruit was bitter, he marked the tree for analysis. This meant the tree was analyzed and studied to understand what was preventing it from producing sweet fruit. Once the workers determined the cause of the bitterness, whether soil, light, water or pests, they'd resolve the issue so the next season it could produce sweet fruit.

When the west farmer made it late to market, the east farmer sarcastically commented, "Your problem is you waste time on the bad trees. Focus on the good trees and stop wasting time on the bad!" He shook his head and chuckled.

As the years went by, the east farmer continued to be the first to market, but the size and quality of his crop remained the same. And he didn't even know why. All he knew was—he had good trees and bad trees. All the while the west farmer's crop continued to grow in size and quality every year.

One day at the market, the east farmer blurted out in frustration, "What the hell are you doing to get a crop like that? Especially with all that time you waste!"

The west farmer replied, unsurprised by the question. "You learn nothing from determining whether a tree produces good or bad fruit. Any fool can do that. No, the secret is in understanding why. Every tree can produce good fruit. It's never the tree that's the problem. Instead, I focus on what is preventing the tree from producing sweet fruit and correct it., so the tree can do what it's designed to do." The east farmer replied with a grunt and went his way.

The next season at market the west farmer said to the east, "I didn't notice the 'big burn' this year."

The east farmer replied with a knowing smile, "Why would I want to burn perfectly good trees?"

I created this parable because it helps paint the picture I believe to be true. I've burned many trees in my life and learned little by doing so. Just like the trees, we're all inherently good and capable of producing sweet fruit. If I label things good or bad, I actually miss the whole point. It's not my job to label something. God didn't put me here to audit his handiwork. I don't think He's relying on me to tell Him whether His creations are good or bad. I've got a pretty good feeling He knows what He's doing. It's not my job to judge, but simply to observe and learn. By judging, I close the door to learning and growth.

JUDGMENT

In the New Testament, Matthew 7:1-2 reads, *"Judge not, that you be not judged. For with what judgment you judge, ye shall be judged; and with what measure ye mete, it shall be measured to you again."*

I once thought this meant, if I was judgmental or unforgiving, God would be the same to me. For example, if I criticized someone for their addiction to drugs, then God would pick one of my sins and be unkind or unforgiving towards me. When you really think about this, does it make any sense? If so, God's saying, *"If you're mean to them then I'll be mean to you."* This opposes everything He's been trying to teach us about how to treat each other.

This is how we as humans tend to work when we are in fear—if that person is going to hurt me then I'm just going to hurt them back. This is NOT how God works.

I now see this scripture differently, especially when I apply the principles of faith and fear. Going back to our example of someone addicted to drugs. If your foundation belief says, *"Man you are screwed and you're going to hell."* Because it's something you believe, don't you have to apply the same thinking to yourself? So the next time you do something you view as a "sin" what is your unconscious belief? *"Man I'm screwed, and I'm going to hell."*

What Christ understands is, the way we judge others is the way we judge ourselves. He's NOT saying, *"Stop looking at others and pointing out their weaknesses or I'll point out your weaknesses in front of everyone else!"* Instead I believe he's saying, *"Don't judge yourself so harshly—don't be afraid."*

If we believe someone addicted to drugs is going to hell. The same fear-based belief must apply to us as well. Fear, at its core, says the Devil's in control. And that truly is a scary thought, because if he's in control of that person through an addiction, then he's also in control of us through our addictions.

This is why I believe Christ is saying, *"Don't judge others OR yourself out of fear. All men are in my hands, including you. Your fear for others is also your fear for yourself. Don't be AFRAID for others or yourself. Thus judge not, out of fear."*

Fear and Faith are energy forms, and we are the conductors. Whatever energy we hold gets transmitted or conducted to everyone we come into contact with. If you're walking around with a heart full of fear, everyone you touch will feel that fear. So going back to our friend with a drug addiction, we communicate our fear, whether we open our mouth or not, because it's energy, and will be felt.

If the fear inside us says, "My friend is lost; I'm so scared for them." That's exactly what your friend will feel from you. If your friend is struggling to hold onto faith every day, and they sense fear from you, it will only sink them further into the grip of their own fear. This perpetuates the drug problem, which is only occurring as a way to mask the pain fear caused in the first place. It's the downward spiral of fear.

All addictions are formed due to a void somewhere in our heart. They all serve the purpose to make us feel better in some way. Whether it's over-eating, anorexia, drug or alcohol addiction, sexual addiction, or work-a-holism, they are all used to fill a need fear says they have. And if we need to feel better for some reason, it's because we're unhappy. Since happiness is a state of mind, unhappiness is caused in one way or another by the illusions of fear.

The scriptures tell us, don't conduct negative energy. In Isaiah 44:8 we read, *"Fear ye not, neither be afraid."* This message is repeated over and over in the scriptures, the great message of peace to ALL mankind.

SEEKING PERFECTION

In Matthew 5:48 we are commanded to: *"Be ye therefore perfect, even as your Father which is in heaven is perfect."* So what the heck is that supposed to mean? Sounds pretty black and white at first glance, doesn't it?

Does God expect us to be perfect, as in, never hurt anyone, never make any mistakes, know everything, and be everything, completely without flaw?

Our typical definition of the word perfect is: without faults, without errors, flaws, sin "in perfect condition". If this is the scriptural meaning, then we would have to be "perfect" at everything we did. A child going to school would already have to know everything before the teacher opened his mouth. A parent would have to know how to "perfectly" handle every situation with her children. A husband would have to be a "perfect" spouse, never saying or doing anything which could be construed as hurtful. In your line of work, you'd have to do everything "perfectly," never making any errors. We'd never be able to get upset, angry, bitter, jealous, proud, etc. Imagine striving to be and do EVERYTHING "perfectly"! The obvious point is—if this is our God's definition of the word perfect, we're all hopelessly lost.

Luckily contradiction comes to our rescue. In Romans 3:23 it reads, *"For ALL have sinned, and come short of the glory of God."* So in one verse He commands us to be perfect, but in another He admits nobody is. Which is it?

The first thing I do when searching for understanding about my Creator is look at the world around me. Since he created this world, where is this perfection He's speaking of? Instantly I find a contrast to man's definition of perfection and his. Man's definition is straight lines, perfect circles, right angles. We look for one right answer as the ruler to measure all others by.

In nature I find none of this. In fact, at first glance this world can look like chaos and disorganization. I can't find perfection anywhere. There's no tree that has a perfectly-symmetrical, flawless trunk. No tree with a perfectly balanced number of branches growing out at specifically mathematically even points off the trunk. No tree with even a perfect leaf! Every one is different in some way.

Let's take water for another example, this is something that chemically is so simple—you'd think if we froze it, we'd get perfect shapes, right? Nope. No two snowflakes are the same. And if none are the same, then how do we define a perfect snowflake?

What about rocks? Don't we have any "perfect" rocks? Isn't there a rock somewhere that's perfectly, mathematically round and symmetrical? Nope. We, as mankind, are so frustrated by this—the first thing we do is get out our levels and squares and begin organizing the "mess". We have to live in homes with straight lines, right angles and set consistent colors. When a wall is scraped or dented, we go into a fit, rush to get the wall patch and touch-up paint to make it perfect again. Or you're at the opposite end of the spectrum and just get mad that it's another eye sore we'll be noticing till the end of time. Either way it's something that is commonly labels as now "imperfect".

Let's face it—many of us are obsessed with perfection. A common core belief is "perfection" is "good". Again, isn't that what we're all struggling for, value and worth? If we can do something or create something "perfectly" then doesn't that make us just that much "better"?

Let's go back to looking at the natural world around us. We don't see perfection in man's sense of the word. But what do we see? Beauty! There may be no such thing as a perfect snowflake, but when you blanket the earth with them it's incredibly beautiful. There may not be a perfect tree, but when you cover a hillside with them it's gorgeous. The first thing we do after making our "perfectly" straight and square houses is put imperfect trees and flowers in our yards. Why? Because they're beautiful!

So if your God's creations show little to no hit of our definition of perfection, then maybe his definition is different than ours. One thing we've already pointed out is—perfection and beauty have no direct connection. So maybe the word *perfect* means something different.

We already know one thing for sure, we're not perfect. But yet there's an unexpected, soothing feeling when we look around at this gorgeous world, which isn't perfect either.

I found another definition of the word *perfect*. The original Hebrew word for perfect is tam or tamim. Unlike our definition, tam means complete, whole, lacking nothing essential. So let's take this and put it into the scripture. *Be ye therefore complete, whole, lacking nothing essential.* Feels definitely different doesn't it? But let's take it one step further. Let's redefine the word *Be*. Again we take this as a command from God as if He's saying "change this about yourself". Which doesn't make sense, why would a God create something and then command us to change it?

I believe the word *be* in this instant means *recognize*. So instead of us being commanded to "be" something different, it's saying *recognize* what already is. Here's the reworded scripture: *Recognize you are complete, whole, lacking nothing essential.* Wow, doesn't that make so much more sense! From a Creator's stand point He's saying, *"I made you whole, complete. Recognize you aren't missing anything."* Be perfect, just as your Father which is in heaven is perfect. Recognize, in my eyes you are perfect and beautiful just like everything else I've created. Most of all, you're perfect just as I am perfect...complete, whole.

Perfectionism from a fearful perspective is a hopeless pit of despair. It's the fear we're not good enough. And it's the most damning of all fear-based beliefs. The fear of not doing something "perfect" is the number one reason for doing nothing at all.

This scripture becomes the greatest tool of faith in that it tells us, *"You're already whole and complete...safe. So now you can feel free to go, learn, do, create and be."*

Faith and fear are simply positive and negative energies we conduct to one another, the parent to child connection being one of the strongest. Everything a parent feels is conducted to the child. God knowing this is making a powerful statement of positive energy by saying, *"I'm not afraid."*, which tells us, we have no reason to fear either.

Looking at this backwards makes it even clearer. If God is scared for us, then by all means it makes perfect sense he'd command us to stop being imperfect. So here's what he'd be saying, *"Stop being bad! Be good like me. Be perfect just like I'm perfect."* But this makes no sense because he's calling himself perfect and his creation imperfect all in the same sentence. How can he be perfect if what he creates is imperfect? How can he be good if his creations are bad?

Thankfully that's not the message. Just think for a moment again about the power of this statement: your Creator saying, *"I'm not afraid for you. I created you perfectly. You ARE perfect, you always have been and always will be."*

No, this isn't a world of two colors, black and white, good and evil; closer to the truth, it's a world of one color—gold, perfection and beauty.

CHAPTER 5

™

DOES YOUR GOD EXIST?

Up to this point, I've obviously assumed there's a God. This is a VERY sensitive subject for most people. Why? Because it's a foundational belief our faith rests upon. When someone starts to "mess with" our belief in God, it can literally shake the rest of our life.

For example, when someone of another faith comes to your door to proselytize, whether they say it or not, you know their purpose is to invite you to join their church. The premise has to be, their church is "better," at least in their minds, than whatever you are doing at the time, whether you attend a different faith or don't attend church at all. Either way, it can make you feel like whatever you are doing religiously is not good enough. Now this type of thing may not bug you if you feel secure in your faith, but for some people, it can make them feel irritated or even angry because this person is touching upon a fear they may have as to whether they're on the "right" track.

Deep inside, we're all seeking God. It's not something we can control, it just is. It's our internal programming. All mankind has a homing beacon which drives us to seek our source of creation or home. It's because we're all driven to find truth. Even someone who may not believe in God is still seeking truth. Scientists are seeking truth. Whatever your pursuit, you'll always be seeking truth. That's how we're programmed. Though he or she may say they don't believe in the God of the Bible, they must claim mother nature, karma, fate, destiny, the universe, the scientific method, or some other god, and give a name to the source of energy within all things.

We have to recognize faith can be fragile, and from my experience, it's constantly bombarded by fear. Believing in a supreme being can only be defined through faith. That's why the scientific method cannot prove the existence of a God, though it can measure His physical laws. We combat the fear He doesn't exist, or He's too busy, or doesn't care. Belief in Him, Her or It, in totality, is a huge stretch of faith.

How many times have we all read into the so-called "good" and "bad" things which are happening to us, wondering *why*? Is God mad at us? Is He happy with us? So many times in our life, we already have fears related to God that if someone begins to do what we feel is poking around in those sensitive areas, we can easily become upset based on our own underlying fears.

For example, let's say I'm struggling to find my own value and worth. I'm questioning everything I've done and everything I am. I'm stuck in fear. I'm feeling or believing I'm lost. And then someone comes to my door from another faith trying to "save" me. In my current state of fear, I'll only see this as more validation that I'm lost and in need of saving. The truth may be that the individual proselytizing is in a perfect place of faith, and their message is pure, in that they are only there to dissolve my fears with the message—you are okay. My point isn't to judge *proselytizing*. It's to understand what our fears are. Whether someone of another faith believes you are lost or not simply doesn't matter. What matters is what YOU believe.

We all are seeking for what our true value and purpose is. We don't need to hear anyone else tell us what we're doing isn't right, or, even worse, we're going the wrong way. That we've joined the wrong church and only one church is going to heaven, and the rest are going to burn. Or there is only so much room in heaven, and you didn't pull a number soon enough, so you're going to burn. This is part of the core fear all mankind has to face at one point or another in their lives.

Fear is only an illusion. The feeling of fear is very real, just like darkness seems very real; however, it doesn't exist in and of itself. Darkness is simply the absence of light. Light, to the contrary, is real, it can be created and controlled. Darkness is not real—it cannot be created or controlled, except through the manipulation of light. Here is where we apply faith to light a dark or fearful subject.

The light side is, we all have faith planted deep inside us. We all want to believe we have good intentions at our core, despite how others perceive us. We can feel this verified by our natural desire to love and be loved by others around us, our desire to feel of value and worth. This is the light that resides within each of us, telling us who we are. The opposition to this light is the dark sections of our heart where our fears exist, causing us to question the light.

Mankind is either born crazy, or there is something real inside each person, driving us in a constant search for his or her connection to a Creator. Every group of people from Adam and Eve, to the Egyptians, the Romans, the American Indians, the Tibetans, the Mayans, and the ancient Greeks, all had their God or Gods. Even when we have found secluded indigenous tribes completely cut off from civilized society, they have formed some type of religion.

The Huaorani (pronounced Waodani) people in the jungles of Ecuador lived in total isolation until contacted by missionaries in the 1950s. They found these people had formed a sort of religion, though it had become a twisted, brutal religion that caused them to live and die by the spear, literally. They instinctively believed in a heaven and hell (black and white mentality), and they believed to make it to heaven you have to "jump the great boa". Yes, as in the snake. Eventually the ministry was able to break through some of the destructive beliefs that were wreaking havoc on their lives, taking these people to a new level of peace and faith. But even in this completely isolated group of people we find the same struggle between faith and fear in search of their creator.

When it comes to any belief, and especially our belief in God, we believe whatever we want to, regardless of proof. For the sake of argument, let's say I choose not to believe there is a God. I would ask myself, can the billions of people who have lived on this earth throughout history all be WRONG?! It's like saying there is a math problem everyone in the history of the world has taken, and in the end almost everyone came up with the same answer.

Let's take the fact we have prophets who've lived on the earth and testified they had SEEN and TALKED to God and were so positive about it, when faced with death, they sealed their testimony with their lives. We could go on and on about scientific proof, historical proof, etc. But NONE of that would matter to me. Because ultimately what I BELIEVE is real. If I say there is no God, whether He exists or not, it doesn't matter, because I'm building my reality without Him. Can you see the power we hold with faith?! By a simple belief, we wield the hammer of construction. And your life will include or not include Him based on a simple belief. **So maybe a better question than *Does He exist?* Should be, *Do I want Him to exist?*** The French philosopher Voltaire said, *"...If God did not exist, it would be necessary to invent him."*

Is the image you hold of God in your mind one that others have created for you; one mixed with fear? Is your view of God something you're NOT comfortable with? Remember the *Trust Your Heart* principle I touched on earlier. If it doesn't feel right, that's because it's not. This God I'm talking about is the One YOUR heart knows, the One YOU are 100% safe with. The One who created and understands you as you are. When it comes to your fear, He knows you better than you know yourself; the One who isn't scared for you, because He, She or It knows the beginning from the end. In the beginning you were okay, and at the end you will be okay. If you're not really sure, don't get hung up on the details, just know, either way you are God's, and God is YOURS!

Why does it just feel right, to believe Something out there created us, Someone is responsible for us? Why do we long for a Source of unconditional love outside of this world; Someone who knows us from the inside out? Why do we want to know there is Someone or Something that put us on the path we're on? Someone who can tell us we are okay, we are all right, in spite of our perceived weakness? Someone who understands us in a way only a Creator could, Someone or Something that knows us better than we know ourselves? Someone who loves and believes in us, when we cannot believe in ourselves? How does it feel to believe this? That feeling of peace and warmth is your inner compass pointing to truth.

Notice how using simple truth and logic are more powerful than any other method of information processing, especially if the person is willing to test it in their heart. There should never be a fight or disagreement between people about the existence of God, because it's between you and your Creator alone. Faith is the proactive force only you have the power to engage. It's a choice that doesn't make you bad or good, because you're already good. It's a choice about what you choose to listen to and what you choose to believe. There are two voices: one communicates fears that we are lost and alone, the other that we are purposeful and loved. This positive voice is your heart verifying truth.

This belief in God is the foundational belief required if you are truly going to use the positive power of faith in your life. I'm not saying you have to go and join a church, BUT you do have to make this choice inside. It's like flipping a huge power switch at the beginning of the faith power grid, allowing you to then have access to that power throughout the rest of your life. This God recognition may be nothing more than you accepting that there is a positive source of energy you are connected to. The simple recognition of this truth will open its power to you.

THE PARABLE OF THE TWO WOLVES

There once was an Indian tribe that sent their teenage boys into the wilderness for an extended period of time as their rite of passage to manhood. The young men would be forced to face their fears, and assuming they survived, would return a man, a warrior ready to take the next steps in his life.

As one young man reached this point in his life, his father took him aside and told him one of the most important lessons of life. *"Son, inside of each of us there are two wolves fighting for control, the white wolf and the black wolf. The white wolf is hope, the black wolf is despair. Whichever wolf wins will determine whether you return victorious or not."*

"How will I know which one will win?" the son asked.

The father responded, *"Whichever you feed the most."*

We make choices every day, to feed the wolf of faith, or the wolf of fear. The foundation to feeding the white wolf is recognizing the existence of YOUR higher power, YOUR Creator, YOUR God.

THE SECRET TO FREEING LOVE

Whether you currently feel connected to your Higher Power or not, I know He's shown Himself to you in some way you can recognize. If you're struggling with your relationship with Him right now, I want you to let go of all the negative that's built up, and focus STRICTLY on the positive.

Focus on the things, and the times where He has shown you He exists, and He loves you. Picture it like a length of cord that may have many knots and tangles in it. Focus on just the beginning of the cord that's not tangled, and on all the other sections that are straight and right. Then have faith the rest will be untangled at some point, but DON'T focus on the tangles. Not if you want to move forward.

One of my personal experiences with this happened when I was in my late teens. I had made the difficult choice to spend the next couple of years serving as a full-time missionary for my church. I then entered an education facility where I would spend a few weeks. At this point, my faith was SEVERELY tested. I had never been away from my family and friends for any amount of time in my life.

As part of the process, I was stripped of all the ego-centered things I held onto as my false sense of value and worth. No longer did I have my own identity; I was just like all the other missionaries, no music, friends, or family. All of the things I thought defined me, such as my skills in working with my hands, restoring cars, my construction skills, etc. were taken from me. I was now the stripped-down version of me, and it felt like I was falling because the sandy foundation I relied upon was washed away.

I began to be overwhelmed by fear and depression. On the one hand, I felt right and good about my choice, but the feelings of self-doubt were becoming increasingly stronger. I didn't believe I could do it; I didn't believe I was "good" enough. The closest thing I can relate it to would be like signing up for the Marines, and then not even being able to even make it through the training exercises. All the fears I'd allowed to exist came in full force to destroy me. One day, I just couldn't take it anymore, the fear inside was suffocating. I didn't want to quit and go home, and I certainly wasn't showing anyone around me I had any problems. But internally I knew I couldn't take it any longer. I found the chance to be alone in the bathroom.

It was really the first chance I had to be alone since I had been there. All I could do was get into a stall, and close the door behind me before I collapsed to my knees. I couldn't pray. In fact, I was so far outside my circle of faith, prayer didn't even seem like an option at that point. I'd never felt this before in my life, as my view of God and myself was nothing but confusion to me. My foundation had been swept away, and I didn't know what to believe or what to do. At that point, due to the overwhelming pressure inside, the words spewed out of my mouth— "Help Me!"

No sooner had those words left my lips than I had the most amazing experience of my life. I immediately felt my body wrapped up as if by massive arms, and a warmth and love penetrated every part of my soul in a way I've never experienced before or since.

The feeling of arms embracing me was so real—I had to look around to see what or who was there. I kneeled on the tile floor as a flood of emotions released, and as joy filled my soul. I felt it say, "I love you." I told Him I loved Him too. And I felt his reply, "I know." I couldn't have been longer than just a few minutes, but amazingly that's all it took. That's the power of unconditional, completely fearless love. I was truly a changed man - not changed from bad to good, but from blind to seeing. Nothing around me changed. My situation hadn't changed in anyway, only my perception of myself changed. And that's all I needed. I left the bathroom and never looked back. I spent the next couple of years learning and teaching others about the love of God. And though, I recognize I was definitely in a state of progression and my efforts could appear very clumsy at times, I did my best to share my beliefs in a way that didn't tear down others' beliefs, but added to them.

Words cannot describe this completely unconditional, absolutely pure and perfect love. It was unlike any love I'd felt before, even different than that of my parents.

Being human, my parents' love could only go as far as their fears would permit them. There is always limitation in mortal love, because it can only extend to the edge of our circle of faith. For example, when a parent embraces a child to love and comfort them, their desire is to tell the child everything is going to be okay, but unfortunately they can only "mean" it so much. Their own fears are saying, "You don't know what your child is going to have to go through. You DON'T really know if EVERYTHING is going to be okay." Fear limits the amount of love that can flow because love is a product of faith; so the greater the faith the greater the love.

This is why the new love I now felt was different. It was limitless! It told me in an instant, everything I needed to know, which was that I was okay and I had NOTHING to fear. I instinctively knew this love wasn't just mine—it was universal! I knew this love was the exact same love He had for every single soul. And in that instant, I felt connected to every other soul, whereas, moments before I'd never felt so alone.

That day in the stall, I left behind much insecurity, pride, and fear. I guess you could say I flushed them down the toilet, because for the first time in my life, I had the REAL THING! I didn't need anything else. My need to compete with others was gone. My need to use my talents, skills, family and friends as my ego crutch was gone. God did exist! I found He loved me, and He loved every other being on this earth, and it didn't stop there! His love was for everything He created, on this beautiful earth, for all of the creatures that live upon it. It encompassed everything. And now all I wanted to do was share that love with everyone around me.

This Being, this Power I felt was not just "my" God. If He created me, then He created all men, and I felt this so instinctively and powerfully. I instantly felt "connected" to all mankind. I just knew we really were one big family. White, Black, Muslim, Jew, Christian, Atheist, all as one. The same God the Muslims worshiped was the same God I worshipped. The God of the Jews was my God also. And though many people might agree this principle is true to an extent, too often, despite this claimed belief, we allow our fears to create boundaries and lines between us. I'm not ignoring the fact we all definitely may believe different things about Him. But those are the tangled sections in our cord of belief that we don't need to get hung up on. The one thing we get to focus on is, we all have the same God. And most importantly, He does exist!

Don't worry if others may believe things about Him that may not feel right to us. That's a tangle in the cord, which will be figured out at some point. And we can't fear it. We're all at different places of progression. Just because a child doesn't understand algebra doesn't mean we should be upset or feel threatened. Hold onto the truths which bring positive fruits into your life. Hold onto the beliefs about your God that feel good and right. Let go of any beliefs about God that don't, at least for right now. Trust your heart, because if you can't trust your heart, then what else is there to hold onto?

CHAPTER 6

TM

YOUR GOD IS GOOD

The fact YOUR God exists is foundational belief number one. The second foundational belief is just as important: God is good. The story I shared in the first pages, where my fears nearly overcame me, illustrated my confusion about God. When things don't seem to work out the way we expect them to, it can cause confusion and fear about God, unless we view them differently. Think of an experience you've had that you viewed as awful. How did that experience make you feel towards God? Did it make you feel confused? Did it make you feel unloved and uncared for? Did it make you bitter or angry towards Him?

There are two issues here:
1. How you viewed what happened to you.
2. How you viewed God as the result of the experience.

Your correct viewpoint of God in these experiences is so important to cement in place in your heart. By so doing, you gain peace, healing, understanding, forgiveness, and most of all, strength! God's goodness is like the needle of a compass pointing north. With that bearing in place, you'll always know which direction to go, spiritually and emotionally!

I'm going off-base here a little, to compare this belief to algebra. Without your knowledge of certain variables, life's equation will look like $X + Y = Z$. In this equation everything is a mystery, everything is up for grabs, everything is suspect (including God), including your own reality. However, knowing God is good is like changing the equation to $X + Y = Good$. As the other variables come into place you can figure the rest of the problem out! It REALLY does make all the difference!

How do I suppose I can PROVE God is good? The truth is I can't, because this is another belief powered by faith. The great part is if you're willing to test it with your heart, the answer is easy!

So why doesn't God just show Himself to everyone and make this a lot easier for us all? If He really exists, what's the big secret? Does He like seeing us all struggle to believe? Is this some type of sick game?

FREEDOM OF CHOICE

The first question I have to ask myself is—when's the last time I asked God to show himself to me? So if I was really going to make the argument God's playing hide and go seek, I also have to ask myself if I really want to see him to begin with. Remember, I'm the creator of my life. God's existence in my life is what I decide it is.

The absolute key to our learning and growth is free agency. By far, it is one of the greatest gifts given to man. Without it, we wouldn't grow. We wouldn't progress. Without it we wouldn't learn how to wield His very power within us, faith. Faith is the fuel that propels us to the happiness we all seek. It's a critical ingredient to our happiness, and it wouldn't make sense for God to take that away from us.

God gives us this freedom of choice, or in other-words free agency. For example, if the presidential election only had one candidate and that candidate was God, would we really be free to choose our leader? No, if God did that to us, it would be a dictatorship, where God knew what was best for us and did it, whether we wanted Him to or not. We'd essentially be controlled by Him.

The freedom of choice is the essence of freedom itself. Because, without the freedom to choose, we lose the ability to learn and grow based on our choices. And note that one of the most important parts is that we get to choose either way. This scares many of us because black-and-white mentality says there's always a right and wrong choice. Free agency is a faith-driven principle that can be scary to us.

Fortunately, this is the way everything is presented to us in life; we are always given a choice as to what we will believe.

The other side of the coin is if we weren't allowed this free agency, it would only be for one reason—because we couldn't be trusted with it. Now I know we've all thought there are times when we really shouldn't have been trusted with it. We perceive decisions and actions as bad or as failures. We wish God hadn't given us free agency and would just help us make all the "right" choices. But this is a false belief of fear. God doesn't have this belief. Instead he doesn't fear our choices, in that he understands that it's all learning and progression, and that's what it's all about for him. He doesn't see any of our choices as bad. He just sees us making choices that lead to a consequence we gain knowledge and experience from.

So God gives us just enough information to be able to choose. And whether we believe he exists or not; it's always a choice. You'll see this balance happen throughout your life; you'll always have the ability to choose faith or fear. No matter how much "good" you see happen in your life, you'll also have just as many things to fear, if you so choose.

A great example is at the birth of my first beautiful daughter Savanna. I was there in the delivery room struck with so many emotions. She emerged, a little, purple, screaming, monster, long, gangly arms and legs flailing, but of course she was precious to me. The doctor laid her in the baby cart. I took her tiny hand in mine and strove to comfort her. As I spoke to her, she instantly began to calm, and that was it, I was hooked for life as I was filled with the new joy of parenthood.

That night as my wife rested I asked that I be able to have the baby instead of her being put in the nursery. I'll never forget that night. I sat in a recliner in the small room where my wife slept. I held our new daughter against my chest, and thought about how my life was now forever changed. I was in love.

In this moment I had an overwhelming amount of things to have faith in; the miracle of this little child God had entrusted to us, she was healthy, she was beautiful, and on and on. BUT I was also presented with just as many things to fear. Remember it's always a balance. It has to be; you HAVE to be able to choose either one. Or it's not agency.

So here's where my fears came in. As I was holding the baby, listening to her little heartbeat, I began to freak out! It sounds so silly but I was getting seriously concerned about her heart stopping. I was so afraid she would stop breathing that I couldn't sleep. I was laying there, torn between how in love and happy I was, and how paranoid I was something would go wrong. My mind drifted to thoughts about how much fun I was going to have as a father, but that was contrasted by the fear failure. I thought about how much I was going to love her, but feared how hard it would be if anything ever happened to her. I thought about how rewarding it would be to take care of her, and yet scared of making mistakes. I felt so incredibly blessed to have her, but scared I didn't deserve her.

This is just one example out of a thousand I could give. Everything in this life must be balanced. Once you understand why—you won't blame God, but thank Him for giving you true freedom.

In this situation, I had to do my best focus on the faith that everything was going to be okay, and ignore fear. I had to place my vote for faith.

With the balance of free agency in mind, let's get back to our "good" God. I did a little research on the word *good* in an Etymology Dictionary, the history of words. I found the word, "good", in old English was actually, originally spelled as "god". But it was just pronounced with a long "o". The words "God" and "good" were actually the same word, originally! And that, I don't believe was by accident. The proof is now in the pudding!

In the book of Genesis, is the record of the creation of the world. In Genesis 1:31 it reads, *"And God saw everything that He had made, and, behold, it was very GOOD."* Why do you think it was important He said that? Did God feel the need to show off? Did he need to pat Himself on the back, "Oh yeah, you DID do good, didn't ya?"

I don't think so. I believe it was written that way because it was important FOR US to know He is the author of everything good. In fact, in the previous verses it states, He saw everything He made, and *"it was good."* He created the light and saw *"it was good."* He created the land and waters and saw *"it was good."* He created the plants and animals and, yes, he saw *"it was good."* As far as the Bible is concerned, this is our first introduction to God. Our Creator knows our natural fears, and in His wisdom, He knew the first thing we needed to learn about Him is, He is the Creator, and everything He made is GOOD.

This is the key to remember: He created everything, and everything is good. He IS good, meaning He is the source of positive energy. He's not capable of creating something bad. I'll ignore that thought you just had about cockroaches, spiders and mosquitoes.

For balance in all things to exist, there must be the opposite of faith, and this is why He allows fear to exist. BUT HE DOES NOT CREATE FEAR! God allows fear to exist, BUT He isn't the author of it. Our agency determines if fear will have power in our lives. God IS good. There is no evil in Him whatsoever.

You may be asking some of the same questions I have, such as, what about God's wrath that's spoken of so many times in the Bible? Does He not get mad at us? One who tells you time and time again in the scriptures to "Fear" Him? Does this not seem like a fearful God? Doesn't it say He has literally taken

His wrath out upon mankind at different times? Wouldn't that be considered negative or bad?

In the Old Testament in the book of Ezra 8:22 it reads, *"...The hand of our God is upon all them for good that seek Him; but His power and His wrath is against all them that forsake him."* Ouch, doesn't that make you feel a little sick? Have you or I ever forsaken Him? How do we know if we have? Are we on His good side or His bad side? What if we have offended Him in some way? The misunderstanding of this and other scriptures can be a source of much fear. Let's say you've come to a place where you feel like you ARE on God's "good" side. You still have to accept a massive amount of fear for anyone else you then have to judge as being on His "bad" side.

Does this really sound like the God you personally know and feel inside? Is He a fickle being who has a temper problem, constantly getting mad at His children for bad behavior? Or getting upset that what He created just doesn't function the way He intended? Isn't this a contradiction to what he tells US to do? What does it say in the New Testament, if someone smacks you in the face, you should get really mad and smack them back harder, right?

Let me repeat the scripture, *"...The hand of our God is upon all them for good that seek him..."* So if you're nice to Him and respect Him and "seek" Him, then He'll be nice to you. But it finishes *"...but His power and His WRATH is AGAINST all them that forsake him..."* So if you "forsake" Him, which we can only assume means doing something that angers Him—then He's going to get mad. I mean, come on, you have the all powerful God, the Creator of this world ticked off at you. What can be scarier?

But does this really make sense? Does this sound like a perfect being? From this perspective, it sounds more like an imperfect being who feels completely out of control of this world, and His only way of trying to maintain it is through threats and punishments. Those of us with kids may be able to relate to this feeling.

But could there be another interpretation? What if, *"...The hand of our God is upon all them for good that seek Him..."* meant for everyone who believes there is a good God, and truly seeks to find that good God in everything, THEN they will find a good God. Their faith will be rewarded, and they'll see everything in their life as good. When I hold this perspective of God in my heart, it's like putting on a pair of yellow lens glasses. All of a sudden everything is bright and warm.

Now for the scary half of that verse, which says, *"...but his power and his wrath is against all them that forsake him."* What does it mean to forsake Him? The dictionary defines forsake to mean: *to abandon, to withdraw companionship, protection, or support from somebody, to give up, renounce, or sacrifice something that gives you pleasure.*

So forsake doesn't mean to do something God doesn't like. It doesn't mean we're doing something "bad" to Him; it simply means to lose faith in Him. Forsaking Him is to pull away from Him, to give up the belief in Him. Wow, doesn't that feel different? Doesn't that make more sense?

But there's one last issue, it still sounds like He is proactively turning on us if we lose faith in Him. *"HIS power and wrath is against all them that forsake him."*

So what's the truth? If we lose faith in Him does he become and angry and begin to use His almighty powers to torment and torture us? If this was true the first question we'd have to ask is why? Why would he get angry? Is he so insecure that our lack of faith hurts his feelings? And how would turning His awesome powers against us make us feel any better towards him?

Logically it makes no sense. So let's look at it from a different angle. Remember that what we believe is true. As god's we create our own world. When we forsake our good God we turn from faith to fear. We go from a state of truth which knows he is good, to a state of falsehood that he is not. A more clear way of saying this is; "For those who believe in a good God they will find and see this good God in every aspect of their lives. For those who believe that God is out to punish them, they will find validation of this belief in every aspect of their lives."

If we lose hope and faith in our "good" God, we'll be overcome by fear. This doesn't mean God needs to go to anger management courses, and most of all it DOESN'T mean we should be afraid of Him, ever. He IS GOOD!

The bottom line is—whether YOU have a God or not is up to you. What you believe is real, or at least becomes your reality. Just remember who and what your God is must become a reflection of you. For you to be good, you must have a God that is. One thing I believe with all my heart—is that mankind is good, and so we must have come from a source of good.

CHAPTER 7

™

WE ARE GOD'S

The next core foundational belief is *we are God's*. Now this actually has two connotations. The first is, we are God's, as in we are in His possession or His creation. The second meaning is we are Gods ourselves, in that we are actually like Him or we have the potential to be like Him. I believe both of these connotations to be true.

Let's establish the truth we are God's children and His creation. But first we must decide, what exactly does that mean? We've already laid the core belief God is good and only capable of creating good. And so, because of that, you are inherently GOOD.

Going back to Genesis 1:26 "*And God said, Let us make man in our own image, after our likeness...*" Notice He didn't just say, "*Okay let's make man.*" He went out of His way to say, "*Let us make man in OUR OWN IMAGE, after our LIKENESS...*" And He said it for a reason. He knew we would struggle to accept who we are, and question whether we were good or bad. He knew we'd be naturally disposed to the fear we were NOT related to a good God.

God wanted us to know we are His. He created you just like Himself. You are part of Him, connected to Him in every way. Every part of you is His; you were skillfully engineered by Him, a miracle science can't even totally understand. From your physical body to your soul, you are a walking miracle. And most importantly, you're good.

Let's revisit this point. He states in verse 31, "*And God saw everything that he had made, and, behold, it was VERY GOOD."* Notice He didn't just say good, either, he said *"VERY good",* just so you and I would understand this important truth. It's ALL good! Including you!

From this verse, notice God's attitude towards everything He does. He looked at everything He created, and said, "It's all good." I don't think I know a single person who truly feels that way toward his or her life on a consistent basis. Especially not me, I tend to rip apart anything and everything I do with my own criticism. Yet God shows us by example how we should view our lives.

Watch out for the trap of thinking, *"Well yeah, it's easy for God to say because He's perfect, of course He can say it's good."* The point isn't that God makes decisions as to whether something is good or bad based on someone's subjective point of view. In fact, you notice He's not asking our opinion. Good or bad is just something we use to label things for our own fearful purposes. So if his attitude is, "It's all good." What should be my attitude? Realizing a black and white perspective is destructive to faith is crucial. Faith says, "It's ALL good."

This goes back to the power God uses to create—faith. Someone of true and unending faith sees EVERYTHING as good. He has no fear, and there's no darkness, it is all light to Him. His standpoint truly is solid, and He sees all things as good. We can place our faith in Him knowing He does know it all, and if He says it's good, then we can put our faith in that, and believe it to be so. What else can we do? Living without faith, we become a ship without a sail or anchor, blown about in the sea of life.

PRIDE, A FAITH VOID

This next core belief is; we are Gods. We have the potential to be like Him. Let's take it even to the next step—omit the word *potential*. Potential means there is some variable in it, as if to say we could be like Him, IF... The only variable is if we actually believe it to be true.

At this point I know what you may be thinking—I'm not trying to say we should take on some false sense of pride or ego about who we are. Actually, I'm suggesting the very opposite. Truly knowing who you are replaces any pride or ego, because there is no need for it anymore. You become filled with the security and an immediate sense of true self value. Just as if you were the son of a king, you'd BE part of the royal family, a king in the making yourself; connected to your father, and thereby a king in your own right. Your Father was the One who put you in that exalted position. It wasn't something you did – or could – do for yourself.

Pride and ego are temporary versions of self-worth. With pride as our source of value, instead of truly believing and treating yourself and others based on the recognition of true worth, we have to pretend like we're something we're not, or in other words we act like we're something we don't truly believe we are. When we accept our connection to God, self-worth will blossom, and fill the void pride and ego were temporary place holders in.

We all have this inherent worth, and we all feel it deep within. However, it is usually buried beneath layers and layers of fear. We fear we are NOT of worth. This creates the conflict that breeds the question, "Why am I of worth?" We begin our lives scrambling to answer this question. We latch onto anything and everything we think could make us more valuable. We find we can obtain this value from "temporary" sources. One way is by comparing ourselves to others. We recognize other people have value, so in desperation to establish our own value, we find areas where we are "better" than they are. The fallacy in this game is if we can't see how we are better than another, then we have to take a step down a rung on the "worth" ladder and go back to searching for something else to make us feel more worthy.

This is what I call building a pride portfolio. It's a group of things that make up our (temporary) worth. It's based on physical and temporal things. Most of my life I've struggled with my own pride portfolio. I'd find temporary security in the way I looked, the things I could do and the things I had. But it's a sandy foundation because all these temporal things are eventually washed away with the tide. How you look changes, what you can do changes as all physical things fade away.

This might sound like a depressing "reality;" however, it's the best part of all. This life is designed to force us to find our true worth. And this true worth is as solid as a rock. I picture myself running across the sand, finding a spot that feels solid, only to watch it wash away. I run to another spot, and another, trying to find solid ground. Eventually I see a spot way up off the beach that's made of solid granite.

This is a life-long cycle we all go through. Please know it's NOT bad. Our natural tendency is to label this as bad so we know NOT to do it. Instead it's a progression and awareness is all we can do to help it along.

I used to believe pride was the "greatest" sin. Proverbs 16:18 reads, *"Pride goeth before destruction, and an haughty spirit before a fall."* I was told and believed pride was the worst sin of all, because it separated us from God and from every other man on earth. Pride is the act of pitting ourselves against other men, comparing and creating our worth by lowering the worth of others. Pride is a bottomless pit that gets no satisfaction out of having something, but only out of having more than someone else.

I began looking for pride in my life, so I could strip it away, but it didn't work, because I saw pride as a "bad thing" in my soul that needed to be rooted out. Pride is a fruit of fear, and because fear doesn't exist; neither does pride. It's like someone telling you darkness is really bad to have in your house, so you need to get "it" out. So you start trying to "get the darkness out". Can you imagine how exhausting that becomes? You can't remove something that isn't real.

It's not possible until you change perspectives. Instead of seeing the darkness as "something" bad that needs to be removed, you simply see a lack of what really belongs—light. When we stop worrying about what's bad in us or wrong with us, we can focus on simply turning on the light and being amazed at how much is right with us!

Like all fears, pride is simply a void of its true filler—our worth as God-beings. I know this cycle well as I tried to "get the pride out". What happens is you feel you've got to tear yourself down in an abnormal way in order to NOT be "prideful", which is working in completely the wrong direction. It's the act of "admitting" your worthlessness.

Imagine the impact of this action. Worst of all it doesn't work—it can't work because it's the same as trying to accept a lie. As long as you're trying to swallow that false belief your heart and soul will be working to reject it.

The only cure for pride is the recognition of your true and unlimited worth as a creator, a worth that is beyond your ability to understand at this point. By shining the light of true self-worth, the shadows of pride began to disappear.

Pride doesn't separate us from God. It's an illusion we fear to be real. Nothing can separate us from God! We are either in a state of fearful belief that we are separated, or in a faithful state recognizing the connection. We're either believing an illusion there is bad in us, or recognizing the truth that we are perfectly in a state of progression. We either believe the truth that we are Gods, or choose to believe a falsehood that we are not.

To summarize this point, pride or ego is the fear we aren't of worth. We all go through the cycle of leaning on pride and ego, until eventually we find our true worth. Again don't focus on the darkness; focus on the light. There's no darkness to get out, only light to turn on. And the best part is it's already there. All the wiring, switches and bulbs are there. You only have to find the switch and turn it on. And even if you see someone else, or you yourself feel like you can't find the switch right now, let that be okay as well. Find peace in the faith that it's there and you'll find it. You're okay right now.

FAITH THROUGH DEATH

As you've seen, there were times in my life where my fears seemed to close in on me. However, life always has balance, and it always gives us the freedom to choose what we will believe, our perspective, our reality, either positive or negative. Here's another real-life experience.

Previous to June 6, 2006, the only two loved ones I lost were my grandparents on my mother's side. They had lived long, good lives, and their passing wasn't a shock to us. Though I felt sad about the loss, I didn't feel too shaken by it. I'd always feared losing someone I was close to. I seen others lose loved ones and watched their reaction. In some cases it had a really negative impact on me. In other words I contracted their fear of death.

June 6, 2006, I was taking my family on an overdue vacation to Florida. We drove through Nashville and stayed with my wife's sister and husband. We arrived late, and I turned off my phone to avoid being woken early. The next morning, my wife came running out the front door to the car where I was unpacking a few things, with the phone in her hand. She had a look on her face I can only describe as scared. She was in a pale state of shock as she handed me the phone, stating it was my older brother, Lance.

"Wade, I have some very shocking news to tell you," he started. *"Dad passed away last night of a heart attack... he's dead."*

The jolt nearly knocked me off my feet. My father in his mid-sixties had better health than anyone I'd ever known; in fact, I'd never even seen him sick. Not one day of my entire life had I seen him sick! Lance gave me the rest of the details, and I hung up the phone. I was numb, not knowing how or what to feel. I knew what I'd seen others feel, but didn't know for sure how I was supposed to respond.

I spoke to my wife for a moment, and then a rush a feelings overwhelmed me. I wept as she held me in the driveway. I felt scared, alone and lost. This man was not only my father, but he was the man who'd always believed in me and my gifts. He was my role model, my boss and my friend. My two brothers and I worked in our family business all of our lives, and now our leader, the president of the company, was gone.

As time went on, I analyzed my feelings. I came to realize two separate sets of feelings. One was the genuine sadness of the loss of my physical relationship, which being completely honest, was replaced with a new type of spiritual relationship that in some ways exceeded our previous one.

The second set of feelings were all fear-based. And these were the ones that hurt. These were the ones that brought sickness to my gut. I learned when someone in your life plays a role of faith for you, when you lose them, there's nothing there between you and your fears. In this case I had fears about my own self worth I was now forced to face. And I didn't like it. This is why I felt scared, lost and alone, because it was my father who gave me much of my self-worth. Now he was gone I was scared the world would "find me out". I would now be exposed for the true failure I feared myself to be.

I didn't see my father as a failure, and because of this, I believed him when he saw me as successful. Up to point I never realized how much I leaned on his faith. And it became the opportunity of a lifetime to get to come to that realization for myself. And that's exactly what started to happen; because I no longer had his physical presence of faith to hold onto, I now had to find it for myself.

What's so crazy is realizing all of the other fears tied to this one, such as; God blessed our business and livelihood because of my Dad. Now that he was gone, what would happen?

As a funny side note, shortly after we'd heard the news, my wife told me she found our 9-year-old daughter, Savanna, sobbing. My wife consoled her by saying, *"Oh sweetie, I'm so sorry"*. Through tears and chocking sobs came her reply, *"Why did Grandpa have to die while we were on vacation?!"*

It's natural to view death negatively. Unfortunately, this view only spreads unwarranted fear and negativity. When someone you love dies, I had assumed, based on what I had seen in others, you fall apart like it's the end of the world . When it finally happened to me, it was like time slowed down, and I was able to open my eyes wide to see clearly both scenarios in my mind. I could give in to my fears and give up on my dreams because my father was no longer there to support me, or I could choose to see the other side.

Initially I had my sweet, tender, loving wife there to comfort me, and then my brother-in-law and very close friend, Brandon, came out and embraced me. I was so blessed to have him with me at that very moment. I went back into the house and spoke with my other brother-in-law, Todd, who offered great words of comfort.

Todd, one of the best chiropractors I've ever known, asked if I'd like an adjustment. This may sound odd for the occasion but in his wisdom he understood the waves of negativity I was fighting and knew how to help me. He not only gave me an adjustment but then performed a pressure point massage while I listened to meditative music. I firmly believe this act was divinely inspired because the massage was so powerfully relaxing and calming. I was completely filled with a spirit of peace and love. It was hard to believe I could be put into a complete state of calm relaxation mere minutes after receiving some of the scariest news of my life. I felt a calming spirit come over me, and as I listened to it, it gave me the strength to see the choice to be positive. I'd NEVER been so relaxed in all my life! Fear and darkness was replaced with love and comfort; should I choose to accept it.

I saw both options clearly. I could push away the comfort offered me, and turn to the fear tapping on my shoulder, beckoning me to fall into its abyss of hopelessness. Or I could turn to the comforting voice saying, "*It happened just as it was meant to happen.*" And somehow, it was all good.

My mother, brothers, sisters and I would go on to have many experiences we could hold onto as special and sacred, again should we choose to. Testaments to the fact my father still lives and is very aware of us; watching over and loving us to this day.

I feel strongly we are loved and directly connected to those who have passed the veil of death. Several months after my grandmother passed away, she visited me. I was on the back porch of our home, hosing it off, and out of the blue, I felt the love of my grandmother. I wasn't thinking about her at all. But all of the sudden I heard her voice in my mind saying, "I love you." It was distinctly her, I just knew it. I could feel her presence, smell her signature perfume, she was there. I still look back in gratitude and amazement.

Here again, I could write about how sad I was at losing my grandmother, yet in reality, she's really not gone. I've felt her, and her love was stronger than in life. I believe it is because she is in a world without mortal fear.

IS MANKIND WICKED?

The fact the scriptures frequently refer to individuals or groups of people as "wicked", has caused me much thought. It seems like unarguable proof people are or can be "bad". If God or a prophet is calling someone "wicked", then it seems pretty clear, right? Here are a number of scriptural passages illustrating this point:

Proverbs 10:3 The Lord will not suffer the soul of the righteous to famish; but He casteth away the substance of the wicked.

Proverbs 11:8 The righteous is delivered out of trouble, and the wicked cometh in his stead.

Proverbs 11:23 The desire of the righteous is only good; but the expectation of the wicked is wrath.

Proverbs 11:31 Behold, the righteous shall be recompensed in the earth; much more the wicked and the sinner.

Proverbs 12:2 A good man obtaineth favour of the Lord; but a man of wicked devices will He condemn.

These passages can superficially seem to be stating that there are good people and bad people, and the Lord takes care of the good and condemns the bad. The question is—is our Creator really calling a portion of His own creation wicked, bad or defective? Can a Good God create something inherently bad? You may think, well no, but maybe we can turn bad based on our own choices and free agency. But that still leaves us with a God that has failed, at least to some extent. If this is true then we must accept that we ALL are participants in this failed production.

The proof stares us in the eye each and every day, in that we all are imperfect, or in other words "wicked" to one extent or another. Technically speaking, (from this perspective) there are none who are righteous. And if there is a "line" separating the righteous from the wicked, then the biggest problem is —no one knows where that fateful "line" between good and evil is. How many sins is it? Is it measured in sins per lifetime (SPL)? Or do we measure it in sins per hour (SPH)? I mean come on; someone needs to create a system of measurement quickly because we are talking about eternal happiness or damnation here. I'm going to need to be able track and control this! Maybe sins per minute would be more realistic when you decide to count sins of omission (sins of NOT doing what you SHOULD be doing). Ugh! It's overwhelming and hopeless when you think about it, right?

In my mind, we haven't found the answer because certain variables in the equation aren't set right. When I look at these scriptures through a different perspective, things seem to actually make sense.

Let's look at the first scripture again, Proverbs 10:3 *The Lord will not suffer the soul of the righteous to famish; but He casteth away the substance of the wicked.* It sounds like God is saying He will take care of the people that are on the "good" side of that invisible line and He'll let the people on the "bad" side starve to death. Notice it says *"the Lord will not suffer the 'SOUL' of the righteous to famish"*. So He's not meaning physically, He's actually speaking of mentally, spiritually or emotionally.

Let's look at this from a Fear vs. Faith perspective. We as human beings have an unconscious tendency to blame God for everything we view as "bad" that "happens" to us. We also tend to give God credit for the things we view as "good". I believe God understands we view things this way and communicates as if He IS the one doing it.

In reality, we are born into a world governed by natural laws, and we are here to learn and work according to those laws. Here He is calling individuals who choose to live in faith, who choose to see things as good even though they could choose to be afraid, as the righteous. The second half which reads, *"but He casteth away the substance of the wicked"* is Him calling those who are choosing to live in fear, the "wicked". So it's not actually the Lord who is doing anything to us—it's simply the natural consequences of the world we live in, based on the way we choose to believe.

Imagine a scripture that says, *"and behold if the wicked decide to jump off the roof of their abode, I the Lord will cause them to fall to the ground and suffer the wrath and indignation of my gravity. And the righteous whom stand by and mock, shall I uphold that they will not be hurt."*

If one guy decides he's going to jump off his roof and his buddy is telling him "You're going to get hurt." Technically the friend is correct. However that doesn't mean the person jumping is bad, and the worst case scenario is he learns a powerful lesson in gravity which he most likely won't need to repeat. There's no such thing as punishment or condemnation, because what purpose would it serve? The natural law by which everything is governed is all that's needed to teach us truth. God is simply stating the natural laws of Fear vs. Faith and what results we can expect based on our belief.

So when people are called "wicked" or "righteous", translate that into faithful or fearful. Understand it's not God judging them, and thereby giving us the liberty to do the same. The point is—we either view OURSELVES as "wicked" or "righteous". When the scriptures say the "wicked" do this, it's talking about the people who view themselves as wicked or in other words those who FEAR they are wicked.

Think about it, we've all been there. We've all had times where we just knew we were complete losers for something we'd done. At that point we were calling ourselves wicked whether we recognized it or not. Numerous times in my life I've thought, *I'm just not worth saving; in fact, I won't allow it!*

In Isaiah 13:11 it reads, *And I will punish the world for their evil, and the wicked for their iniquity…* This is totally true in that, when I am in my fearful state over my own "sins" I am severely punished, but perhaps it's not as it seems. God isn't standing there with a whip beating me. It's ME beating myself. Remember he uses natural laws to govern all things. We receive the consequences for all our choices, either faith-based, or fear-based. Just as the guy who leaps from his roof, and learns about the natural law of gravity, we learn about the natural laws of living in fear or faith. The consequences come to us thru the natural laws, not by some wrathful Being, whom we've offended.

This also makes even more sense when you compare it with seemingly conflicting scriptures such as John 3:17 *For God sent not his Son into the world to condemn the world; but that the world through him might be saved.* Viewing these two opposing passages in fear, sounds like God can't make up his mind. Are we wicked or righteous? Are we saved or lost? Which is it?!

God claims that Christ has paid the price for sin. This is also a natural law God orchestrated for us all, because in the end, who is or isn't evil? He makes it perfectly clear the price He paid was infinite and it was for ALL mankind, right? We are saved by faith, right? Then righteousness isn't a lack of mistakes or a higher level of perfection than others, it's a belief everything is going to be okay. That you yourself are okay and others are okay, despite the state of imperfection we are in. It's more than even a belief. It's recognition of truth; tested in the heart.

Haven't you found this to be true in your own life? You've had times when you just wanted to not exist anymore because you were so disgusted with yourself. What was the only way you were ever able feel better? Was it because you somehow became perfect and therefore no longer had to feel bad about yourself? I don't mean to make assumptions but I'm assuming…not.

At some point you had to let go of the fear that was fruitless and had no end. Fear is the emotional state of hell spoken of which is a never-ending fire that can't be quenched. The only way to stop the pain is to walk out of the fire, to let go of fear and take up faith. It's the only solution.

As long as we live, we will see things we can choose to be afraid of, whether we are old or young. We can choose to fear ourselves and our weaknesses, we can choose to see our "wickedness" or we can choose to see our "righteousness". We can choose to see the God within us, or fear the Devil within us. But the one thing we must know is our Creator KNOWS who we are. This life is not a test for God to learn who we truly are; it's a test to teach US who we are. This life is for us, not Him. It is for us to learn and grow and to choose faith over fear, to learn to use the power of creation innately within us all, the power of faith.

The scriptures are asking us, "What do YOU believe? Are you wicked or righteous? And what will you believe about the people around you as well? Are they also wicked or righteous, despite their outward appearance?

We are God's, and if we truly are created by Him and He is good, then all mankind is good at their core, and now we know what the answer is in our algebraic expression when we are dealing with ourselves and others. $X + Y =$ Good.

Earlier, we examined the relationship of the words Good and God. I also believe it was no accident the word *Gold* is so similar to these as well. One of the definitions I found for gold was: *Something regarded as having great value or goodness: a heart of gold.* Gold is our standard of worth; it's commonly what we use to create wedding rings, signifying our eternal devotion to our spouse. It's what the most valuable currency was minted of in the past. It's what we give as the highest medal in the Olympics, to signify one's worth as being the very best. I believe the word gold is very closely related to the words God and Good not by accident but by intention.

When you use the term "heart of gold" I want it to mean something different to you. I want it to be real. I want you to know being the children of God means we do have a heart of gold, or in other words a heart of good. We use the term "heart" to signify what we think is the true core of us. It's what we picture our Creator as the author of. So when we speak of who we truly are at heart, it's the same as saying, "Who are we really inside, if someone could cut through all of the fear?" We must believe all men are good, that we are God's.

CHAPTER 8

TM

MANKIND - THE TAPESTRY OF GOD

A further extension of the "We are God's" theme is the fact we (mankind) are all connected. We are all brothers and sisters, created by the same Source. I once had a superficial belief that said, "Yeah, we're all related, great." But when it really came down to it, I didn't realize how very profound these connections truly are. It's like saying you're related to your 3rd cousin Billy, who you've seen once. This connection seems to have little effect on your life.

I hope to show you how genuinely connected you and I are to ALL mankind and the serious impact that can have on how we view things in life. It can make all the difference in our level of faith regarding others, and ultimately ourselves.

The message to love our "brother" is a major theme of religion. Why is that? On the surface, it seems that to be a "good" person I just need to be nice to other people. I now have a slightly different perspective that feels more accurate to me. I believe we are all connected in a very real and powerful way. The best example is we are like a fabric, each of us a strand of thread woven together in the tapestry of mankind; the Creator being the Divine Weaver. Whenever there is an impact on one individual, the ripple flows through the rest of mankind. Let me give an example of what I mean.

When we watch the news and we hear of something tragic that happened to someone else, what happens to us? We feel something, don't we? We feel empathy for the person we view as the victim. Why is that? We feel empathy toward other human beings for a very real reason. We are all a part of one another, one entity, one being, all a part of the body of mankind. We cannot hurt someone else without feeling the pain ourselves, and we cannot hurt ourselves without hurting others around us.

Now let's look at the other side of the coin and consider when we see something good happening. One way we can measure what someone is feeling is by the endorphin levels in their body. Science has found endorphin levels increase significantly when an individual performs a kind act for someone else – physical proof they are feeling good at that moment.

But what's even more interesting is that same physical reaction happens even when we are just VIEWING someone else doing something kind to another person. We don't even have to be involved to get that good feeling! You know what I'm talking about. When you're watching *Extreme Home Makeover* or some other show displaying acts of kindness from one person to another, you can't help but feel good!

In fact it's a joke between my wife and I. Somehow we're always trying to eat dinner while watching *Extreme Home Makeover*. And, all of the sudden, we look at each other and start cracking up because there is some touching story happening and we're trying to eat and not cry at the same time!

The fact we are affected both positively and negatively by merely witnessing other individuals illustrates how positive and negative energy flows through the fabric that connects us all.

When you see a news story of one person hurting another, we know how we feel toward the victim, but don't we also feel something toward the aggressor? In fact, some people have made it their life's work to understand individuals who have committed awful crimes against others. Why do we care?

Deep within our soul, we all have a connection to each other, and when we see someone do something awful, it "messes" with us. We feel anxious and concerned because of that connectedness. Therefore, seeing a horrific act or just hearing about it sends our mind into a problem solving spree. We first check the act against our belief system as to whether mankind is all good, or partly good and partly evil. If we believe people are black and white, then this decision is fairly easy, we throw the perpetrator into the "evil" pile and try to move on. If we believe all men are good, then we struggle to understand how something like this could happen.

Here's where the good/evil, black/white mentality becomes a two edged sword. The problem is the person who adheres to this dualistic, polarizing principle must also apply it to himself and his loved ones, as well as to every other human being. He is forced to confront some fearful questions: if that person was able to be evil, then I must somehow be capable of the same? And who else around me is evil, or could turn evil at any moment? What about people I love? For example, if it was a spouse who hurt the other spouse, you might ask, could *my* husband/wife ever be capable of that or could *I* be capable of that?

This is when you realize the black and white view of mankind doesn't make sense and it's miserable to live every day in fear. So we stuff that whole situation in the "To Be Figured out Probably after I Die" pile and try to move on. But that can be the very problem; this belief system is damning and prevents progression.

I GET MY BUTT KICKED

As a 16-year-old, I attended a high school in which there was an elevated level of violence. My best friend Mike and I rode the bus to and from school, and we began to have problems with some of the other guys on the bus. It started one day when Mike, being a bit on the obnoxious side, was making cat-calls out the window to a girl. A big kid jumped up, slapped Mike in the back of the head, told him to shut up and sit down. Mike did so, but not without defending himself with some smart comment. Over the next couple of days things began to escalate. A friend of the instigator came up to me at my locker and said he was going to "Kick my butt" when we got off the bus, so Mike said, "Cool, we'll just get a bunch of our friends and fight back!"

That day riding home on the bus was, for me, one of the most scary days of my life. I was not a "fighter" and had avoided it most of my life. These other guys seemed pretty comfortable with it. Mike wasn't helping the situation either. He had finally told one specific individual that he was going to fight him. And so being a "good" friend, I unloaded with Mike at this other guy's stop to see the two fight. My heart began to roar in my chest when nearly the entire bus unloaded with us. My guess was they weren't there to stop anything. We were outnumbered by at least 5 to 1, despite Mike having a carload of his friends waiting there when we got off the bus, which I found out later they had even brought guns. But they had decided things were getting too out of hand, (thank heavens) and left moments before the fighting erupted.

It started with the typical trash talk, and as we were encircled, it was expected Mike would begin fighting this one guy. Just as I began to realize what was happening the kid who'd threatened me at my locker punched me straight in the nose. I erupted in a fit of fury, kicking wildly at his head. He either ducked, or I just missed badly. I was out of control for a few seconds and then regained my composure and thought, *No, don't do this, Wade, you'll regret it.* I also realized I probably was going to be beaten either way so I didn't need to stoke the fire anymore than we already had.

Mike was now well into his fight with this other kid. He seemed to be holding his own at first, but wore out quickly, and soon the other kid was sitting on Mike's chest, pummeling his face. Mike was laying there, bleeding from his nose, eyes and other places and I really began to get really concerned.

But at this point Mike cried out for my help. For a split second I had to pause. I knew the fight was, up until this point, a "fair" one-on-one fight, and if I were to interfere, it would mean all "rules" would be off. However seeing no other option at the time, I reached out and grabbed the guy who was re-arranging Mike's face by the shoulders.

The boisterous crowd was instantly upon us. I began to be beaten from what felt like was every angle, and fell into the fetal position. In a split second everything went black. I'm not sure how much time had passed, but I woke up next to Mike.

As things came into focus, I saw everyone scatter as a police car pulled up. I looked around and saw my brother Lance arriving. He jumped out of the car and ran towards us in a rage. The officer warned Lance not to antagonize the aggressors. So instead he helped Mike to the car. Mike threw up in the street before getting in. We answered a few of the officers' questions before taking Mike home. When we got to Mike's house, his parents called an ambulance and he was taken to the hospital to be treated for head wounds and miscellaneous bruises, cuts and abrasions.

I went home, not having the amount of injury Mike had sustained, and laid on my bed. Physically speaking my back was what hurt the most. But what shocked me the most was realizing that emotional pain hurt far worse. Being a kid, I didn't understand why, but what hurt the most—was my feelings. It sounds weird, but if I'm really honest the truth is I felt SO VERY AWFUL inside, not just at the guys beating us up, but at the situation.

You know how you feel if you have a bad encounter with another person? It can be someone you don't even know cutting you off on the highway. On the surface, it can make you mad, REALLY MAD. And you have a hard time letting that feeling go. Why? Why do we care especially since we don't even know this person?

It's as I said before: we are connected to every other human being, and when we experience negative energy between ourselves and someone else, it is felt. We cannot feel hurt without others feeling it. And we cannot hurt others without feeling the pain we cause them.

OUR CONNECTION

This situation created the biggest rift or negative shock in my connectedness to man I'd ever experienced in my young life. It's hard to describe the experience of having another person so apparently angry at you they physically beat you unconscious. And it was my feelings that hurt the most. It was like someone saying they hated me, multiplied a hundred times. Once again, I had to ask myself, eventually, "Why do I care? Why can't I just forget about these guys? I didn't know them really—I only saw them on the bus. But deep inside I couldn't HELP but to care. And I couldn't resolve my feelings towards them for years afterwards, until I finally accepted the fact I was connected to them, and the only way of healing was to understand where the pain came from.

If we are all connected together and connected to God, we cannot separate ourselves from another person without separating ourselves from God. For example, I spent years filled with hatred and anger towards these individuals. And as much as you try to label another person as evil and try to throw them out, you still are left with the disturbing fact that whatever (or, more accurately, Whoever) created you, also created this "evil" person. At best, this is extremely confusing. At worst you're filled with anger towards the individual and God.

I mean, He's the Being who created the kids who beat Mike and I unconscious. In reality, I was pretty upset God let me get hurt in that way. And I showed it through my anger. The bitterness began to consume me, and I remember one night sitting in a restaurant with my older brother, Lance, and some other friends. As had become a habit, I made a comment about the fight again, trying to be funny, but being more bitter than anything else. Lance looked at me and said, *"Ya know what? I'm really getting sick and tired of the person you're becoming. All you do is spew anger and bitterness about the guys who did this to you. You're not enjoyable to be around anymore. Are you going to let that one experience ruin your entire life?!"*

Wow! That was a real wake-up call for me. I was shocked to realize what I had allowed to grow in me and knew I had to stop it, because it was robbing me of happiness and peace! For a period of time, I'd even started kick boxing, with the fantasy of getting revenge one day. I allowed fear to consume me so nearly that all my free thoughts were of revenge. I never rode the bus to school again and changed many other aspects of my life based around that one event. I slept with a knife under my mattress and a BB gun under my bed. (I know, I know, what was I really going to do with that? It just supports my point, fear is completely irrational) And the one thing I unconsciously had to accept, was that in order to ever "beat" these other guys, I'd have to be more scared than they were--more bitter, more angry, more violent.

FAITH AND FORGIVENESS

I remember as a child in Sunday School having a lesson on forgiveness. The teacher had us put a tiny pebble in our shoe and walk around the room. As we walked she explained how being unwilling to forgive was like having that pebble in your shoe. I remember the feeling going from really uncomfortable to intolerable, quickly.

I've thought about this often. I believe it's fairly common knowledge that forgiving feels better than holding a grudge, but here's where we know the "what", but what we need to know is the "how". How can you take that pebble out of your shoe? Because we've all been there it may seem easy to say, just forgive the person who beat the tar out of you. This doesn't usually work because it's focusing on the symptom instead of the problem. You're trying to get rid of the effects of bitterness without understanding the cause. From this standpoint it's nearly impossible.

So, realizing these events in our life separate us emotionally from our fellow man, how do we reconnect? The first thing we have to find is the cause. What was causing me this pain? The first fact we must understand is that happiness and pain are feelings that come from within NOT from the outside. What this means is that it's impossible for someone to hurt you emotionally or spiritually from the outside.

Now you may be thinking, "That's a stupid thing to say. Of course someone can hurt you emotionally. It's easy. All they have to do is say something hurtful to you, especially if they're someone you really care about."

Let's say it's true. That being the case it means you and I are subject to the whims, moods and decisions of others. How does that feel? It feels pretty scary. The thought that anyone out there has the ability to control my happiness makes me feel out of control. It makes me feel like I'm a victim instead of a creator. Most of all it doesn't make me feel good. That's my first clue it's false.

Here's a different perspective. Others can only verify fears we already have about ourselves. For example if a stranger walked up to you and said, "I don't like you." It would feel most likely, unpleasant. The natural response would be to tell them how you felt about them at that point...not good. But what's really going on here? Why did it hurt? It can only hurt if there is some fear INSIDE of US that believes we aren't always liked by others. So we have a fear somewhere that others don't like us and someone validates this fear by saying they don't like us. When you have matching negative energy you experience a small negative explosion of emotion. Remember, however, that the part in this equation that matters is that part that lies within you. Just because someone else is experiencing great fear still does NOT give them control over you.

Let's say for comparison that we don't have the fear that others don't like us and this stranger walked up to us and claimed they didn't like us. We'd actually be able to see clearly what was going on. We'd see that since all emotions come from within and NOT from without that this individual was feeling un-liked by others. Because he or she feared or believed this they were acting and creating based on that belief. They were working to validate their own fears by injecting you with their negative energy. But since you didn't have that matching fear within yourself it had no where to go. You're also now in a place of power to see and help this individual re-write a false belief with truth by telling them, "Well I like you."

Though I've used this example to display a point I'm not suggesting you dig out all the fear in your soul this moment, thereby protecting yourself from pain. It doesn't work that way of course. My point is to teach you, when you're hurt, know it's coming from somewhere inside. Know that it's tied to a fear somewhere. A fear you can have full control over to re-write. And when you do the pain goes away.

In my case with these other guys, it all went back to my core fear. I've always had a deeply rooted fear that forced me to question my worth. Being in high school at that time this fear was enflamed as nearly all of the other kids around were struggling with the same. We're all searching for value and worth.

Because most everyone in high school is insecure, it's a cycle that breeds more insecurity or fear. Riding the bus, we could smell the fear in the air day after day, and finally one day there's a spark. That's all it takes and the group of us went up in the flames of anger. The other guys were no different than Mike and I. They're just looking for value and worth as well. And due to the situation they felt they could "get it" by taking away ours.

Isn't that what fighting is all about? We're fighting for our value and worth. As men we commonly believe one very clear and simple way to measure value is by physical strength. We gave them an excuse and opportunity to gain or validate their value by pummeling us.

Consequently, what we felt them saying was, "You're a piece of garbage that we're going to take out! We are stronger, better, smarter, faster, or in other words "good"; which is also saying to us we were weak, dumb, slow or in other words "bad". It was as if they reached into my soul, found my deepest fear of myself, pulled it out and waved it in front of my face and the world. I watched in horror as they played judge and jury to declare me guilty of being a loser. As hard as I'd fought to find my own self worth, it seemed, they'd taken it away from me in a matter of minutes.

Not only did they send us away beaten, but a group of them drove by Mike's house to laugh as he was put into the ambulance! Talk about facing some real fear.

But what really hurt about it? Physically am I still in pain today, of course not. The physical pain was gone within days. So what was the pain that went on for months and even years? It was emotional pain caused by the matching fears we both had that we were of little worth.

When I really define the pain, what hurts most is the fear I had of myself which I saw them validating; the fear that I WAS a loser. This is where my pain came from. And unconsciously they were counting on that fact. They themselves had the same fear. Believing I had it as well, they knew exactly how to reach into my soul and use my own weapon against me. And at the time it worked.

However, stepping back it becomes clear. There's no pain because that which I feared to be true—isn't. The pain instantly leaves and is replaced with peace. I have no need for revenge, because first of all, I am not hurting. Second, I can see clearly what their real issue is—their own personal fear. Why would I need to attack someone who is only acting in a state of false belief?

In Matthew 5:39 it reads, ...*resist not evil; but whosoever shall smite thee on thy right cheek, turn to him the other also*. Now this statement actually makes sense. Previously I believed this to mean when someone causes you pain, you just let them cause you more pain because that's the "right" thing to do. But that's not it at all. Instead He's saying, "resist not evil (or fear) because it's not real." If someone "smites thee" which means they make a statement of fear against you, realize it's not real. And if you truly let go of your fear, no longer will it hurt. You can turn the other cheek because it doesn't hurt or shouldn't hurt because it's not true!

What causes the pain is our belief that the negative they're communicating is true. When someone flips you off on the highway, it may tick you off. If so it's because of what you believe about it to be true. We become defensive only if we believe there to be some truth in us they are pointing out. If someone calls you a jerk, it only hurts if you believe there is some truth to it.

This is not to say we don't do things that can be interpreted as bad. I've been distracted while driving and actually ran someone off the road. Luckily it was just onto the shoulder and no one was hurt, but they weren't happy about it. The natural response in this situation is to feel "bad" about what I did. To feel bad in this situation means I need to recognize the fool I am for doing that. Unfortunately this leads you down a road of fear. It becomes about "who" we really are. It goes back to judgment. It becomes another check mark on the "black" side of the score board against us.

Instead I just have to recognize it happened. See it NOT as something that define me negatively but simply a cause and effect. When I do this I get that. I don't want to run someone off the road, so I'll no longer do what I was doing that distracted me.

Forgiveness is most commonly believed to mean we "forget" about something "bad" we did. It's like shoving things in a closet we do our best to ignore. But this isn't true forgiveness, and all we end up with is a closet bulging at the seams. One day you're going to try to stuff one more thing into the closet and it's all going to come crashing out in an awful, validating display of all the "bad" things you're "capable" of doing.

Real forgiveness is recognition of the heart of gold we all have. Because deep inside we never do have "bad" intentions, technically nothing you do is "bad". I know that's hard to grasp. We all are our own worst enemies, and sometimes we think it feels good to beat ourselves a little for the "bad" things we do. But in the long run, feeling bad about ourselves means we are generating negative or false energy, which is then what we have to conduct to others around us. You can't beat yourself up without beating everyone you're connected to as well. Picture trying to beat just one strand of thread in a tapestry with a bat.

You can't feel bad and not conduct it to the people connected to you. Your only choice is to feel good! Isn't that good news!

I want to summarize the core beliefs we've discussed so far:

- Your God Exists
- He is Good
- You are His and so is all mankind
- You are Good, and so is all mankind
- You are inseparably connected to all mankind and to God
- And IT'S ALL GOOD!

CHAPTER 9

™

HITLER VS. DISNEY

Ding! Ding! Round one begins. Okay now I know you're asking yourself: "What?!—is this some kind of Celebrity Death Match Extreme Edition?" And what's the point? We all know who's going to win if this is about violence.

This is something I've thought long and hard about, and I believe will prove a powerful example of the powers of fear and faith. I realize we need to test the Core Belief, all men are good. As I stated in the beginning of this book, when I realized I had some very fundamental things backwards, I had to work out in my mind where the kinks were. I realized, as hard as I tried to believe I was good, something kept pulling me backwards. For some reason I was resisting TRULY believing this. I came to realize it was my black and white mentality. It was the elementary way I viewed myself and others as either good or bad. And as long as I believed that, I was ALWAYS fighting to prove my goodness and worth. I was constantly fighting to earn my ticket to heaven. And it never worked. In the end you're left endlessly struggling with your fear.

I heard a story once about a religious leader. He was concerned about the lack of faith amongst his flock, so one Sunday, as he addressed the group, and asked a question. *"Who here believes, without doubt, if they were to die right now they'd go to heaven. Please raise your hands."* He was shocked. Almost no one responded, it was like he struck a nerve and nothing but feelings of confusion, frustration and fear arose. He thought to himself, *"What are we all doing here then? We come to church every Sunday, we work and work and work to keep the commandments and do the things that 'make us good people' but still the end result is NOT achieved!"*

If nothing else, this is THE goal of religion. To increase the faith of the members so they believe what is already real. They ARE GOD'S! Instead, sometimes church turns into the "Goodness Tryouts", and those who pass, go on to paradise. But the ironic part is nobody meets the criteria, no one who's playing that game ever wins. You can't win at it because it's not real.

What I mean is, if you work at trying to prove how good you are, you'll always fail because that's completely opposite to the very nature and purpose of this life! We were put here to LEARN. It's like my son going to kindergarten trying to prove he already knows everything. He would actually fight AGAINST learning in that state. And quite honestly, that's what I spent much of my life doing. It had a damning effect limiting my learning and growth, because I was too busy being afraid of not being good enough.

What do I believe the answer is? Part of it is throwing away the "Black and White Theory", (as it applies to people) and taking on the "Gold Theory". Meaning men are not good or bad, but are God's, and they are therefore connected to a never-ending source of good. The only way to believe this—is for you to believe it to be true for ALL mankind. Why is that? How come we can't just say, "Well, there are quite a few evil people out there, but I refuse to believe I am. I will stand firm on the fact that I AM GOOD." It's because IF someone else CAN BE EVIL, then you HAVE to open the same possibility to yourself. And once again you are back on the Black and White train, going for a never-ending ride.

Okay, okay I know what you're thinking now, "But, but, but what about this really, REALLY EVIL person I saw on the news who did all of these awful things?! How on earth could that person be good?! How could God have created such a monster! How could God allow that monster to exist and treat others like that! I have a hard time understanding that!"

Daring to go through that door to leave the black and white room I've spent my life in was difficult, but I had no other choice. I had to know and understand these principles that were so key to my peace and happiness. I had to answer the questions: Are we really good or bad? Can we as people be evil? Do I have the potential to be evil? My heart told me the answers were "no" but I needed to understand why. I decided I would have to take the man I viewed as the most evil man who's ever lived and see how the principles of faith and fear worked in his life.

I needed to understand what happened there. If God created Hitler, and God is not capable of creating evil, then what the HELL happened?! How can this newfound "good" way of believing possibly relate to such an outwardly "evil" man?

I know it's hard to even concede, but remember that for me, if I couldn't see the "God" in him—If he was evil, and by evil I mean like as in the spawn of Satan, then I still have to concede he was created from the same source I was, and there was a possibility I could become or uncover that same evil within me. And the same fate was possible for all mankind, assuming the conditions were right.

So I began researching the person whom I felt was responsible for the death of the most innocent lives in the history of the world. This person's actions led to the deaths of more than 6 million Jews. He was responsible for the murders of over 3 million Polish citizens, and 2 to 5 million others, including Romanians, his own German people who were physically handicapped or mentally retarded, as well as psychiatric patients, homosexuals, Soviet prisoners of war, Jehovah's Witnesses, Adventists and Neopagans. Not to mention any political opponents or members of resistance groups. Of course, you already know who I'm referring to—the notorious Adolph Hitler. All in all, estimates of 50 MILLION people perished in WWII just in Europe alone! Not to mention those deaths attributed to other dictators across the globe doing similar things in Japan, Italy, and Russia. The wars of fear waged during this time claimed nearly 70 million lives worldwide. What amazing far-reaching negativity.

It's not difficult to prove Hitler's negative effect on the world. And I think universally we believe him to be an evil individual. Maybe even a child of hell—meaning someone whose heart IS truly evil. How else can such unspeakably evil results from one individual be explained?

Before I go any further, I want to clarify my intentions. This is a very sensitive subject, more sensitive to some than others, but one which I don't take lightly. It is not my intention in any way to justify or validate any of the atrocities of this man. My intentions are in fact quite the opposite. I want to show how I believe these things came about for two reasons. First of all, if we understand and learn from the mistakes of history, we may be able to prevent them from being repeated in the future. Secondly, I hope that understanding may bring about some healing, not just from the specific acts surrounding this individual, but the same principles may be applied to the "Hitler's" currently in each of our lives.

What I found in my studies of Hitler absolutely amazed me. I wasn't sure at first what I was going to find, but finished with peace and understanding. In the past, living a black and white life, I was afraid of "bad" people, like it was a disease, as if they were infected with the Devil and it was contagious. I would never venture to research an "evil" individual, for fear of contracting his evilness. And although fear is contagious, "evilness" is not.

When one individual fears another, they have to throw morality out the window and do whatever they believe they have to in order to protect themselves. Right and wrong become completely subjective. If someone can be evil or "bad", what is the "right" thing to do? Get rid of the "bad".

In a fearful state of mind I would not have wanted to learn anything about Hitler for fear I would be traipsing around the Devil's property and he might see me and suck me in. This all was an illusion, an illusion to keep me out, to keep me in ignorance and fear, because knowledge is light and darkness can't exist where light is.

There are endless books written about Hitler. But to avoid the opinions and paradigms of others, most of what I'm using comes directly from his own words in his work *Mein Kampf*, which means, *My Struggle*, written by him when he was imprisoned for thirteen months for being a leader in an illegal mass political demonstration.

After my analysis of Hitler, I'll be comparing Walt Disney. The side-by-side comparison brings many truths to light. I'll obviously be giving my insights and opinions on what I've read and digested. I do not, however, claim to be an expert on the historical events surrounding these two men. My purpose is not to give a history lesson, but to illustrate how two men with nearly identical childhoods could turn out so differently. I'll begin with Hitler then go into Disney and then summarize both; it's going to be awesome!

CHAPTER 10

TM

HITLER - EVIL INCARNATE OR THE ULTIMATE CULMINATION OF FEAR?

Hitler was born April 20, 1889, as an only child in a small town in Austria. His father was abusive verbally and physically to both he and his mother. But his mother, Klara, having lost three children previous to Adolph, was very loving and caring of him. Hitler mentions his great love for her and was known to carry a photo of her wherever he went throughout his life. When Adolph was 5, Klara gave birth to his younger brother, Edmund.

His father, Alois, was the illegitimate son of Maria Schicklgruber. It is believed by some she became pregnant while working as a servant for a Jewish family named Frankenberger. That seems to be further supported by rumors the 19-year-old Frankenberger son regularly sent money to Maria after the birth of Alois. Whether this is true or not, it seems Hitler was very sensitive and insecure over this, based on some of his later actions. As a leader, he passed a law, making it illegal for German women to work in Jewish households, and German blood to marry individuals of the Jewish religion. He also turned his father's hometown into an artillery practice area.

Alois left his own home at the age of 13. It seems he was embittered towards his family and surroundings, and left to "prove" his worth. After many years of struggle, he finally achieved the position he had set his sights upon, that of a civil servant working for the Austrian government. He returned to the village of his upbringing to be hailed for the man he had become, but was completely invalidated as the village had changed and no one even remembered him. It seems the cycle started here as his father struggled to find value and worth, another way of saying he FEARED he had none.

Not long after Alois's first marriage to Anna, he had an affair with 19-year-old Franziska, who became pregnant with Alois's first son, Alois Junior. It seems Alois Sr. took out his bitterness on Alois Jr. who at the age of 13 ran away from home and eventually ended up in jail for theft. Here you see the pattern repeat itself.

After two failed marriages, Alois married again, this time to Klara Polzl. Having "failed" as a father to this point, Alois seemed all the more determined to do it "right" this time, and make Adolph a success.

I can only get the impression from my reading Alois was much like myself or anyone else I know, in that we tend to look at all of the things we've done as a long list of failures. We become fearful that we ARE truly failures, and this fear breeds a deep anger. This fear displayed itself in violent spouts of abuse as Alois tried to "correctly" raise Adolph.

However scary this may sound, I can relate to some of these feelings. As a young father I remember being scared of everything such as being a good father, being a good husband, being a good person and supporting my family. I remember wanting to please my wife, and us desperately needing furniture for our new home. So after MUCH discussion, we went to a furniture warehouse (which was the cheapest place I knew of to find furniture). We ended up buying, on credit, a fake leather recliner that would be comfortable for my wife to rock our young children.

I was stressed about this, and pretty much all other purchases. I felt like we really did need these things, but I didn't have the money to pay cash for them. I was taught this was a big no-no, and felt very scared I was doing things the "wrong" way which made me feel bad about myself. Not too long after the purchase, I remember coming into the family room to the sight of my 2-year-old with a pair of scissors in her hand, now I'll let you have one guess as to what she was doing...

...Yeah, she was "customizing" our new, fake-leather chair. The same chair I'd put on credit! You probably can relate. So what happened? Of course all of my fears culminated into blind fury. I spanked her in anger and threw her into her crib. I storm out of her room slamming the door behind me.

Eventually I calmed down and logic began to take over, I realized it's just a chair. I started to understand the fear lying in wait just under the surface for such an event to set me off.

The bottom line was I didn't want to feel that way. I can't stand feeling negative, bitter and angry, and I don't know anyone who enjoys it. I know a lot of people, including myself, who can't help it at the time. Buying the chair wasn't a "bad" thing to do, but my fear of being bad because of it, created a situation that brought my fears to life, and I did end up doing something I really believed was "bad". So with regretful tears, I went into the nursery, and stood at the crib of my sweet little girl. Through my emotions I said, *"I'm so sorry."* She replied immediately by jumping up and wrapping her arms around my neck, instantly and completely forgiving me. Thank heaven for a child's faith, which gives them the incredible power of forgiveness.

When you live and breathe negativity inside, it can only come out in negative actions. On the other side of the coin, I've never known a person who's looked at their child from a perfectly balanced, neutral perspective and said, "You know I really feel like I need to hurt my child today. I think that would be a great activity, I don't really have anything else to do." No, it all stems from fear, negativity and insecurity inside, which can burst out at any moment in fits of anger and violence.

Think about the word "insecurity" for a moment. All of us are insecure about something in our lives. But what does it really mean? One definition of the word insecure is: *deficient in assurance; beset by fear and anxiety*. Being insecure is being scared. It's a lack of assurance we are okay. I see this fear in Alois and watched it be transferred to Adolph, as you'll see.

BOYHOOD

As a boy, Adolph loved to play cowboys and Indians. Like most young boys, he became entranced by the conflict of black and white mentality. When I say most young boys, I'm meaning we start out young defining good vs. bad. What boy hasn't played cops and robbers, cowboys and Indians, etc? We're born with a deep inner goodness, but as fears develop, this gets twisted into WANTING to be good, and in wanting to be good, someone has to be bad, right? We actually have to find the evil to prove our goodness.

During this time in Austria and Germany, books by James Fenimore Cooper and Karl May told tales of the American West, which became very popular. Adolph loved these books and read them over and over, even through his adult life as the Fuhrer. The hero in Karl May's books was Old Shatterhand, who always won his battle against the Indians with sheer courage and willpower. As the dictator of Germany, it was said Adolph would refer to the

Russians as "redskins". He even ordered his officers to read these books.

Hitler was intelligent and did very well in his early years in school so that he had a lot of free time. He spent much of it enjoying the outdoors. He was a natural-born leader and claimed to be the ring leader among the "rough" kids locally which made his mother very anxious at times. He was also "rather difficult to manage" at school.

Ironically, in his free time he liked to sing in the choir of the monastery church at Lam Bach. He states he was so impressed by the magnificent splendor of the ecclesiastical ceremony that he looked to the Abbot, the head of a community of monks, as the highest human ideal worth striving for. This is his first mention of his search for value and worth. Here he sees the religious leader as the ultimate calling. He told his father he wanted to become a priest, and his father refused the idea. It seems his father was very critical of Adolph's perceived talents. He mentions his father viewed him as a stubborn trouble-maker and made it clear any religious career for him was a major contradiction. In other words, Alois told Adolph you have to be a "good" person to do something like that. Notice how the fear Alois had of himself which was "I'm not of worth" was transferred to Adolph, and steered him away from the possibility of becoming a priest.

This is a very common fear that gets transferred from parent to child. If the parent fears himself not capable of something, then how could he have faith for HIS child to be able to succeed in that area? For example, if Alois feels like a failure as a parent, then Adolph will never get the approval he's seeking for himself as a parent from Alois. Because how could Alois see Adolph as a successful parent when he wasn't himself? It wouldn't make logical sense he could raise a son to be a successful parent when he himself was a failure.

This experience turned Adolph to another direction, which he says was "better suited to my temperament". He found among his father's books one about the Franco-German War of 1870-71, and this became his favorite reading. Anything that had to do with war and military affairs become his passion. His cowboys and Indians now turned into battle re-enactments and he was so enthusiastic about these games he would wear out his neighborhood friends playing it, and have to find other boys to play with.

A FATHER'S FEARS

Adolph began drawing lines between good and bad (black and white) at this young age. This was not unusual if you keep in mind we all tend to draw the lines between bad and good as we try to find self worth. He also states that not soon after this point in his life, he began to feel a deep patriotism for what he fervently believed to be the "Motherland", Germany. Since he is living in an Austrian-held part of what used to be Germany, he began to draw the line between Germany and its "enemies" as good and bad, in this case Austria being the country he resented. He states in his own words, *"German-Austria must be restored to the great German Motherland."*

At the young age of 11, Adolph was forced to face death for the first time when his younger brother Edmund died of measles at the age of 6. Adolph was shaken badly by this event. Edmund was buried in a cemetery next to their home, which Adolph could see just outside his bedroom window. It is said Adolph could be found at night sometimes, sitting on the wall of the cemetery, staring off into the night sky. I have no doubt Adolph was at that point in his life asking some serious questions but not feeling like he was receiving many answers.

At the same time Adolph was proving to be a talented artist and based on several strict requirements with his other studies, his father agreed to enroll him at the Realschule, a school that could help develop his talents. It never occurred to Alois this could develop into anything more than a hobby.

Yet just a year later, Adolph determined he had found it, he knew what he wanted to be -- he was going to become an artist. He expressed this determination to his father. His father's reply was to exclaim, *"Artist! Not as long as I live, never!"* This became a bitter argument between the two.

This being one example of Alois's verbal abuse, his physical abuse was highlighted when, as an adult, Adolph recounted to his secretary, *"I then resolved never again to cry when my father whipped me. A few days later I had the opportunity of putting my will to the test. My mother, frightened, took refuge in front of the door. As for me, I counted silently the blows of the stick which lashed my rear end."*

Alois had fought through his fears, or so he thought, to become a successful man in his own eyes. This was no doubt a scary experience for him, and, like all parents, our natural "good" or "gold" heart tendency is to want the absolute best for our children, however, our fears translate that good desire into something else. For example, Alois knew how hard it was for him. Things didn't come easily, so naturally he was very scarcity-minded. This made him determine that the best, or maybe the only way, for Adolph to make it in this world, was for him to follow the same line of work he had spent his entire life creating. He also felt like he could possibly pull some strings to give Adolph a boost, and hopefully Adolph would be able to be even more successful than he had been.

Notice how his very limited faith can't see any other possibility of success for his son, except through the gut wrenching path he had taken. You can also see how this would affect Adolph. His father was basically saying, "I barely made it, and I greatly fear you won't make it." It's no doubt Adolph was thinking, "I'm going to do whatever is the opposite of what my father did, because there's no way I'm going to end up like him."

This is communicated in Adolph's own words in the first chapter of his book *Mien Kampf*, where he writes, speaking of his father, *"Probably also the memory of the hard road which he himself had traveled contributed to make him look upon classical studies as unpractical and accordingly to set little valued on them. At the back of his mind he had the idea that his son should become an official of the Government. Indeed he had decided on that career for me. The difficulties through which he had to struggle in making his own career led him to overestimate what he had achieved, because this was exclusively the result of his own indefatigable industry and energy. The characteristic pride of the self-made man urged him toward the idea that his son should follow the same calling and if possible rise to a higher position in it. Moreover, this idea was strengthened by the consideration that the results of his own life's industry and place him in a position to facilitate his son's advancement in the same career."*

Let's analyze this quickly; Alois had good intentions, meaning he was a "good" person, with that heart of gold. However, his fear blinded him to what Adolph's talents were, and his fear communicated something very fundamentally life-changing. His fear said to Adolph, "You're NOT good enough to succeed with the God given talents you possess. Most likely you WILL fail, the only way you'll have a chance in this world is if you use as leverage what I've done in my life. Because nothing comes easy, it's hard, really, really hard."

This stemmed from Alois's fearful perspective of his life. He viewed all he had as something he had to forcefully take and claim for himself, because life was a struggle. This view says if there's a God, he's not a bountiful God, and He's not giving handouts; at least not to me. You have to out-smart Him or go "around" Him to get the things you need in life. It's a scarcity mindset that says: there's just not enough to go around.

When Adolph was 13, his father, Alois, died suddenly. In his own words, Adolph recounts, *"When I was in my thirteenth year my father was suddenly taken from us. He was still in robust health when a stroke of apoplexy painlessly ended his earthly wanderings and left us all deeply bereaved. His most ardent longing was to be able to help his son to advance in a career and thus save me from the harsh ordeal that he himself had to go through. But it appeared to him then as if that longing were all in vain. And yet, though he himself was not conscious of it, he had sown the seeds of a future which neither of us foresaw at the time."*

From this statement, I imagine Adolph to have mixed feelings; one side I don't think was sad to see him go. I imagine a weight was lifted from him by the loss, something he wouldn't want to necessarily admit in a political book. However, I do believe there is also some truth to the other side of his feelings that he would be sad at the loss from the perspective that he did truly understand his father's sincere desire to help him. He could see his father's good intentions. But I don't think the seeds he mentions his father sowed were the seeds of faith. Instead Adolph inherited the fears of his father, the seeds of fear, and insecurity.

Let's take for example a child and a hot stove. If a child touches a hot stove, immediately he is burned for an act of faith he showed by simply trying to learn what the thing was, which was glowing red.

Now the child has two choices as to how he or she will deal with this experience. He can view it fearfully, which will cause him to fear touching things in the future, in which learning and progress will be slowed, and he can become more insecure about the world around him, fearing a world filled with things to hurt him. He'll see the stove as a punishment and therefore see himself as bad for touching it. This bad feeling will turn into bitterness towards the stove, and anyone around this child who doesn't see the stove as "bad" will make the child feel insecure. The child will feel that if others don't feel as they do about the "bad" stove then, maybe in some way they are on the "stove's side." The child won't understand the difference in views and will feel invalidated, frustrated and slightly alienated by those "stove loving" individuals. Fear is the source of conspiracy theory.

Now let's look at it in contrast from the perspective of faith. This child has just touched the stove and was burned in consequence. Keep in mind it is faith in the first place that gives children the power and fuel to learn. They go about touching EVERYTHING. Trust me, I have three children, it can be very frustrating, BUT it's how they learn, grow and progress. So how should they view the stove that burns? The laws of faith say, "It's ALL good!"

Here's how the child in this situation could do this. I imagine an adult being there to help facilitate this learning. The adult takes the child and addresses the wound, then explains that the stove is a wonderful thing, its heat isn't designed for the purposes of hurting, but it's a tool to cook delicious, nourishing foods for our enjoyment. By touching the stove, you just gained valuable knowledge that will help you avoid misusing this tool in the future. Eventually you'll learn how to use it to cook as well. So you see the stove is really a wonderful thing. The very thing you fear about it being bad is actually good. If it didn't get hot we couldn't make delicious foods.

This example may seem overly elementary but the same principle applies even in one of the world's greatest tragedies. We ALL have insecurities born of fear. But a parent, especially a father, is the foundational figure in a child's life. And when that foundation is built on fear the child learns there is much to fear.

Imagine a child witnessing a lightning storm. It's natural for them to fear it. The adult normally has knowledge of this, and their faith is a positive energy a child can feel raising their negative, fearful energy to a higher level. But picture a child seeing lightning and hearing thunder, then looking instantly to the parent, to verify if there is cause for fear and the parent freaks out, screaming and shaking with fear. The child goes into cardiac arrest. Faith and fear are energy forms just like electricity, and we as people are the conductors of that energy. We cannot help but feel the positive or negative energy of others. And a child is a perfect conductor of energy. In many cases they will assume the positive or negative energy of the adult.

So as children absorb fear from a parent, they grow up believing there is A LOT to be afraid of. This tends to turn into a never ending conspiracy theory. Everyone has it "out" for this person, and they tend to feel invalidated and even afraid of those who don't buy into their conspiracy theories. They end up making most of their decisions based on these fears and their true progress and growth is stunted. Worst of all, their ability to love and accept love is severely handicapped.

I want to qualify this by repeating: EVERYONE has fears. And ALL parents communicate fears to their children, mostly unconsciously. I also want to remind you HAVING FEARS DOESN'T MAKE YOU BAD. It makes you normal and natural. Fear shouldn't become the new "bad", meaning we start using the term fearful for someone "bad" and faithful for someone who is good. That's opposite to the point. No one is bad; we're just all at different levels of faith. And that's okay.

STRUGGLING TO FOLLOW HIS HEART

Adolph's family moved often when he was young and though he did well early in school, by the sixth grade his performance dropped and he had to repeat the grade. At this age, Adolph began showing signs of depression and insecurity. His teachers reported he had "no desire to work"; and at age 16 he dropped out of high school.

He was determined to follow a career in what I believe he felt was his only talent. He left his mother, who was then becoming ill, to go to Vienna to apply at the *Academy of Fine Arts* to become educated as a painter.

In his own words, *"I felt convinced that I should pass the examination quite easily. At the Realschule (Adolph's High School) I was by far the best student in the drawing class.... Therefore I was pleased with myself and was proud and happy at the prospect of what I considered an assured success. ...I was so convinced of my success that when the news that I had failed to pass was brought to me it struck me like a bolt from the skies. I went to see the Rector and asked him to explain the reasons why they refused to accept me... He said the sketches which I had brought with me unquestionably showed that painting was not what I was suited for but that the same sketches gave clear indications for my aptitude for architectural designing."*

I find significance in the words *"it struck me like a bolt from the skies"*. This may have been a simple statement he makes without much thought but seems to imply he felt struck by Mother Nature or God, in this most devastating event in his life to this point.

So let's discuss for a minute how he must have been feeling in his relationship towards God and his fellow man. So far we know his home life was unbalanced at best (keeping in mind there is NO such thing as a "functional" family or in other words a perfect family). He did receive love from his mother, but his relationship with his father was built on fear, which showed itself in the form of confrontation and bitterness.

Through my reading I also got bits and pieces that later in school, Adolph was somewhat of a loner. He had a tough time communicating with others and did not make friends easily. We also know that as an adolescent, he showed signs of depression, not a big surprise—any adolescent in this situation would struggle with security. You have a father at home telling you your talents are worthless, you don't make friends easily, and move frequently on top of that. Still, you may be thinking okay, but that's not really all that abnormal, and definitely not an excuse for killing millions of people. And you're right; it's not abnormal at all. In fact, today we have adolescents in the same situation, and given the right circumstances, they've actually taken out their rage on others around them, even to the point of violence. So why is this?

When an individual begins to feel badly about themselves or are afraid they are worthless, the pain becomes unquenchable. Everyone has insecurities, but those are usually balanced by the love of friends and family. Kids at school will always be cruel, out of ignorance and immaturity combined with fear, but most kids have a support system that helps them through these trials. But when you combine the following three factors:

1. We all naturally lean towards fear, the fear of ourselves, that we are not good enough
2. Not having a balancing support system of love and faith
3. The relentless negative input kids can give each other

You have a formula for disaster. These kids initially are confused, they have something inside telling them they are loved and of worth, but without outside validation, the negative forces of fear can become suffocating. Eventually, they'll begin to feel everyone around them stands as a witness of their worthlessness. The fear builds to the point where they feel attacked on every side. Fear paints evil faces on the people around them, and drives them to insanity.

What I mean by insanity is there's scientific proof that when a person is feeling fear, their level of adrenaline goes up. When your body reaches a certain level of adrenaline you physically are no longer capable of rational thought, making you at that point temporarily insane. You're physically incapable of making reasonable logical or sane decisions. So fear literally can and will lead to insanity, however temporary.

Another reason why fear in this situation is so confusing to the individual is they feel the very real conflict inside. They feel their own worth and connectedness to man and God. Remember, they have a heart of gold, or of God. But they receive information externally telling them they are alone, separate, worthless. The two sources of information create painful confusion. "Which is it?!" the victim must think, "Am I valuable, or worthless?" The fight, without help, becomes exhausting and the answers to the insanity become extreme.

Back to Adolph, who after his devastating failure at the *Academy of Fine Arts* tries again to pull himself up and determines to take the advice of the Rector and work toward architecture. Again he hit a brick wall as the fact that he dropped out of school meant he couldn't enter a tech school for architecture since he had no diploma. His own words are, "*...I was quite crestfallen. I felt out of sorts with myself for the first time in my young life.*"

"*Within a few days I myself also knew that I ought to become an architect. But of course the way was very difficult. I was now forced bitterly to rue my former conduct in neglecting and despising certain subjects at the Realschule.* (beating himself up over the fact he'd dropped out of school) *Before taking up the courses at the School of Architecture in the Academy it was necessary to attend the Technical Building School; but a necessary qualification for entrance into this school was Leaving Certificate from the Middle School. And this I simply did not have. According to the human measure of things my dream of following an artistic calling seemed beyond the limits of possibility.*"

So often in this life our greatest fear is we don't deserve to live our dreams. And trying to, is the scariest thing you'll ever do. I know. Living your dream means following your heart. And following your heart means you open your chest to the world, believing deep inside that what and who you are is good enough. The scariest part is the fear it's not; because IF it's not, it means YOU'RE not—not good enough. It's like pulling out your soul to be judged and laying it all on the line. You fear you've got a 50/50 chance of success. Either they stamp it good and you are set for life; or they stamp it BAD. And what that means is unfaceable.

This is only an illusion of fear because as I've stated, we're ALL good. But to follow our heart means we face our core fear, the fear we inherently are not "good" enough.

So if there's anyone who believes living your dreams is bogus, here's one powerful situation where I think we ALL wish Adolph would have lived the dream he had here! In fact it's heart-breaking to watch him come to accept the lie of fear that he wasn't good enough to live his dream.

Going back to just before his failure at the Academy, Adolph convinced his mother to allow him to drop out of school and apply at the Academy of Fine Arts. About this he writes, *"...my mother agreed that I should leave the Realschule and attend the Academy. Those were happy days, which appeared to me almost as a dream; but they were bound to remain only a dream. Two years later* (Adolph being 18 at the time) *my mother's death put a brutal end to all my fine projects. She succumbed to a long and painful illness which from the very beginning permitted little hope of recovery. Though expected, her death came as a terrible blow to me. I respected my father, but I loved my mother."*

Adolph's mother died of breast cancer. It was recorded he sobbed when the doctor first diagnosed the problem. They determined she needed immediate surgery. Despite the surgery her condition worsened. She spent her last days in a bed in the warm kitchen of their home where Adolph kept a constant watch over her, taking care of all the household chores and tending to her needs. She apparently bore her pain well, but Adolph was torn to pieces over her condition. Eventually she passed on December 21st amidst the Christmas season. Hitler was devastated. The Jewish doctor, Edward Bloch, said he'd never seen anyone so overcome with grief as Adolph was at the loss of his mother.

This becomes more sad proof of Adolph's faith deficiency. If there is anything in this life we must handle by faith, it is the loss of a loved one. His reaction to her passing shows how out of control and lost he must have felt. For he had lost everyone close to him: his father, younger brother, and now his mother. His loneliness and desperation must have been very real. His deep affection for his mother is even transparent in his intimate description of Germany being the "Motherland".

It's not hard to understand what any person would be feeling in this situation. Adolph's only source of good was, as he saw it, taken from him. He was now left to himself. Notice how he even speaks of the happiest time of his life as just a dream. He didn't even believe it when it was happening. His fear wouldn't allow him to accept good even when it was happening. It seems the seeds of fear his father planted were beginning to sprout as Adolph started to see these "bad" things happening.

It's also important to realize the ONLY way someone deals with death in a healthy way is through faith. There's just no other way. This is meant as no criticism but his difficulty dealing with her death is another sign his faith was nearly non-existent, at least in that scenario. The pain involved with the loss of a loved one is not the loss of their physical presence; if this was the case, we'd freak out every time we were parted from them. No, the real cause of this pain is the fear we didn't deserve them in the first place.

Adolph begins a downward spiral, but still strives to hang onto some small shred of faith, in his own words, *"Poverty and stern reality forced me to decide promptly. The meager resources of the family had been almost entirely used up through my mother's severe illness. The allowance which came to me as an orphan was not enough for the bare necessities of life. Somehow or other, I would have to earn my own bread. With my clothes and linen packed in a valise* (a small piece of luggage) *and with an indomitable resolution in my heart, I left for Vienna. I hoped to forestall fate, as my father had done fifty years before. I was determined to become 'something'..."*

We can see from the words Adolph uses what he is feeling. Notice he says, *"with an indomitable resolution in my heart"*. Here's the positive side we talked about before, the heart of gold. He's feeling some amount of faith here that he's worth something and the fact he uses the word heart tells us it's a sincere core feeling. This is the faithful side still struggling to work through the fear; but notice immediately after that he says, *"I hoped to forestall fate, as my father had done"*, showing the other, fearful side.

If he has to "forestall fate" it means he believes fate has already written him off as a failure; and he needs to do something to change it. And what is fate? Is it not also God? Adolph is looking at all the "bad" flowing to him and feeling angry, bitter and confused towards God. He also says, *"as my father had done fifty years before"* which confirms the fear based belief his father communicated to him. His father had to "forestall fate" because God wasn't going to help him out either. He had to take what he needed because God isn't going to give it to you. You have to fight for what you need.

Adolph ends with the comment he was determined to become "something". This may not seem like a big deal, many of us might use that term, but looking into what that says is important. He viewed himself as worthless at the time. Now this may not seem like a big deal, but these are all little brush strokes that help us see the bigger picture.

What Adolph didn't understand was he WAS of worth to begin with. All he had was his mother to instill that in him through her love. When someone loves us, we feel lovable, which means we have worth. Just as the greatest life changing event for me, was feeling God's love for me. It made me feel the most complete form of worth a person can feel. It is THE source of true worth. Knowing there is an all-powerful God that believes you are worth loving. This instantly changes your perception of every other human being. You cannot help but see their worth as well, knowing innately they are loved just as you are. And though Adolph did feel love from his mother, and his actions show how desperately he strove to hold onto that one and only love, it seems it just wasn't enough to hold back the tide of negativity and fear.

From here, Hitler begins the creation process using the force of fear. This perspective changes everything, instead of seeing the things you need coming to you, you see yourself having to forcefully take them. You see negativity all around you, and though it may be with good intentions, you begin to act in desperate and irrational ways.

You do not see God as the source of good, but you see Him as a heartless onlooker. If you want or need something you must take it. The law of the jungle applies to this way of thinking: eat or be eaten, my loss is your gain, it's a dog eat dog world, etc. This is in complete opposition to the truth of our connectedness; it makes one feel completely isolated and alone fighting against the world. Most of all, this belief makes one feel unloved and worthless as Adolph himself seems to be admitting.

"After the death of my mother I came to Vienna for the third time. This visit was destined to last several years. Since I had been there before I had recovered my old calm resoluteness. The former self-assurance had come back, and I had my eyes fixed on the goal. I would be an architect. Obstacles are placed across our path in life, not to be boggled at but to be surmounted. And I was fully determined to surmount these obstacles, having the picture of my father constantly before my mind, who had raised himself by his own efforts to the position of a civil servant though he was the poor son of a village shoemaker. I had a better start, and the possibilities of struggling through were better. At that time my lot in life seemed to me a harsh one; but to-day I see in it the wise workings of Providence. The Goddess of Fate clutched me in her hands and often threatened to smash me; but the will grew stronger as the obstacles increased, and finally

the will triumphed."

This paragraph again shows Adolph's two wolves of faith and fear fighting for control. On one hand he's trying desperately to muster his faith and courage to move forward, but he's doing it based on a weak foundation displayed by his last comment, the "Goddess of Fate" threatened to smash him. The fact he feels like he is being punished by God and he has to work against Him, or Her in this case, is clear.

This is not some abnormal feeling, however. It's probably one of the most common feelings man can have. I know these feelings all too well, it's why I'm writing this book. Naturally, if man is left to himself, he will gravitate towards fear and negativity but through his contact with others, through loving relationships and positive interactions this is balanced out. Notice I didn't say it's completely done away. Because it never is, we will always feel the balancing power of fear not far from us. Just as night comes, fear will always be a part of our lives, but it's like climbing a mountain. We overcome fears every day we climb, and even though we still have more to climb, we can also look back at all we've overcome and thus feel the blessings of hope due to progression.

Adolph was going through a very normal situation and dealing with very normal feelings we all can relate to in some way. Remember, I'm not saying because Hitler is normal, what he ended up doing was not very negative. I'm trying to illustrate that the awful negative his actions brought about came from his very normal negative thoughts and feelings.

THE FINAL BLOW

Hitler then went through what I call the final fearful blow. For the next five years he suffered through complete poverty. And because of the "fearful preparation" he's already had…it embittered him to his core.

I'll share some of his words about this period of time. *"For many people the name of Vienna signifies innocent jollity, a festive place for happy mortals. For me, alas, it is a living memory of the saddest period in my life. Even to-day the mention of that city arouses only gloomy thoughts in my mind. Five years of poverty…in which first as a casual laborer and then as a painter of littler trifles, I had to earn my daily bread. And a meager morsel indeed it was, not even sufficient to still the hunger which I constantly felt. That hunger was the faithful guardian which never left me but took part in everything I did. … I was always struggling with my unsympathetic friend. … During those years a view of life, a definite outlook on the world took shape in my mind. These become the granite basis of my conduct at the time. Since then I have extended that foundation only very little, and I have changed nothing in it."*

Here I believe what he means by this last comment is during the most awful time of his life he formed his perspective and view on life. Now imagine if you took the hardest part of your life and wrote your foundational beliefs based on it; meaning you based everything you believed on something negative. He says it becomes the "granite basis" of his conduct! Not only that, but he never saw the positive in it; his fear is truly cemented into place in his heart.

An important exercise we must all go through is to see the good in even the hardest events of our lives. Hitler becomes only embittered by it, and sees it as more proof for the sake of fear. It's a classic downward spiral you get caught in, and can be very difficult to get out of.

Fear says everything is bad, and so you look for the bad around you. When you look for bad you find it, everywhere. Not only that, but you also begin the creation process, for the negative. Remember, fear is simply faith going in the wrong direction. You use this creative power for the building of more negative. You can only create from the power that is predominately inside of you. If you feel predominately negative feelings, then you'll produce predominately negative results. If you feel predominately good feelings, you'll produce predominately good results. This is a simple law of nature that can't be broken. It is the same laws God abides by and uses to create good. In this case, Hitler begins the creation process using the foundation and powers of fear and the results are truly destructive.

He goes on to talk about what happens to a person who has to struggle from complete poverty to an average working class status. *"In the case of such a person the hard struggle through which he passes often destroys his normal human sympathy. His own fight for existence kills his sensibility for the misery of those who have been left behind."*

This is such a classic statement of fear, which says it's the survival of the fittest. At the same time, you can see Hitler still recognizes the "normal human sympathy" he had lost and I can't help but feel he says this with some remorse. I believe he felt as I have in many situations where my fear got the best of me. I knew what I was doing out of fear wasn't positive but didn't know how to stop. And Hitler is absolutely right in that fear DOES disable our normal human sympathy drowning it out.

From what I've learned through my study, Hitler, will not achieve a level of balance again during his life. He didn't have another positive loving relationship until later on in his life, long after his fear has cemented itself into place. It would be with Eva Braun, his girlfriend who stuck with him to the very end.

Remember one of the core beliefs of faith is we are all connected. In opposition to this is the core fear; we are alone and disconnected. This feeling of separation is made even more evident as Hitler talks about poverty in the following words, *"There was hardly any other German City in which the social problem could be studied better than in Vienna. But here I must utter a warning against, the illusion that this problem can be 'studied' from above downwards. The man who has never been in the clutches of that crushing viper can never know what its poison is. An attempt to study it in any other way will result only in superficial talk and sentimental delusions. Both are harmful. ...I do not know which is more nefarious; to ignore social distress, as do the majority of those who have been favored by fortune... ...or the equally supercilious and often tactless but always genteel, condescension displayed by people who make a fad of being charitable and who plume themselves on 'sympathizing with the people.' Of course such persons sin more than they can imagine from lack of instinctive understanding. And thus they are astonished to find that the 'social conscience' on which they pride themselves never produces any results, but often causes their good intentions to be resented; and then they talk of the ingratitude of the people."*

Since fear says God does not or will not give you what you need, when an individual with this fearful belief sees others with more than he has, what must he then think? Obviously, God favors others and not him. This leads to confusion, feelings that others must be "good" since they are so blessed and we are "bad" since we aren't. This thought goes against our heart which tells us we are all good and God is good, but since we can't reconcile these feelings, our natural defense mechanism, which is anger, kicks in. We become angry and bitter towards others who have more; because we believe it to be a sign or reminder of our worthlessness. God loves them more than He loves us.

Adolph shows these sentiments in a classic way drawing a clear line between him and the "upper-class". He bitterly criticizes the "rich" for condescending to give to the poor as if it's just a fad to be charitable, and that they "plume" (a token of honor or achievement) themselves on the fact that they sympathize with the poor. He then even calls what they do a "sin" because of their ignorance. Notice how hard he has to try to make them look bad. Why? Because they are that symbol that says he is bad. As his only defense, he calls them bad in order to regain some of his own self-worth. He feels this desire so strongly he's writing a book about it!

You can also see his anger is not simply about money (or lack of it). If it was just about money, and he was the benefactor of financial support, his anger wouldn't be directed at the rich class. But instead, he even says their "good intentions" are resented; meaning that even when they give, the problem for him isn't fixed but actually is made worse. This is because his problem isn't poverty, it is fear. And when these people he already fears are "better" than him give to him, it makes it even harder to rationalize they are "bad", which is his way of feeling "good". So he must rationalize away their good actions as evil.

It's quite the predicament; he fears he's worthless and finds proof in the fact that he has nothing. He sees himself as worthless since his talents and skills are on lockdown by the goddess of fate, and since the only people of value in his life have been taken from him.

This is NOT true, of course. Fear never is based on reality. His perceptions could have been totally different, and he could have made different choices. Many others have suffered tough circumstances in their early years, and still chosen to find the bright, or true, side of things. This scenario in his mind of the rich looking down on him was nothing more than his own fears that he was "less than" they were. Whether they thought that or not doesn't matter; what matters is HE believed he was less than they were.

I feel like I understand this because I've felt the same way at times in my life. Despite the fact I've never had to suffer with hunger, I still managed to feel bitter at times towards others who had more than I had, because of my own insecurities born of fear.

The following is a montage of Adolph's feelings at the time. Here you'll see what he was basing his life perspective on.

"I soon found out that there was some kind of work always to be got, but I also learned that it could just as quickly and easily be lost. The uncertainty of being able to earn a regular daily livelihood soon appeared to me as the gloomiest feature of this new life that I had entered.

In most cases (an individual) comes to town with a little money in his pocket and for the first few days he is not discouraged if he should not have the good fortune to find work. But if he finds a job and then loses it in a little while, the case is much worse. To find work anew, especially in the winter, is often difficult and indeed sometimes impossible. For the first few weeks, life is still bearable. He receives his out-of-work money from his trade union and is thus enabled to carry on. But when the last of his own money is gone and his trade union ceases to pay out because of the prolonged unemployment, then comes the real distress. He now loiters about and is hungry. Often he pawns or sells the last of his belongings. His clothes begin to get shabby and with the increasing poverty of his outward appearance he descends to a lower social level and mixes up with a class of human beings, through whom his mind is now poisoned, in addition to his physical misery.

Then he has nowhere to sleep and if that happens in winter, which is very often the case, he is in dire distress. Finally he gets work. But the old story repeats itself. A second time the same thing happens. Then a third time; and now it is probably much worse. Little by little he becomes indifferent to this everlasting insecurity. Finally he grows used to the repetition. Thus even a man who is normally of industrious habits grows careless in his whole attitude towards life and gradually becomes an instrument in the hands of unscrupulous people who exploit him for the sake of their own ignoble aims.

I saw this process exemplified before my eyes in thousands of cases. And the longer I observed it the greater became my dislike for that mammoth city which greedily attracts men to its bosom, in order to break them mercilessly in the end. I was thrown about so much in the life of the metropolis that I experienced the workings of this fate in my own person and felt the effects of it in my own soul."

Though speaking as though he watched many other people go through this, you can see he's clearly speaking about himself. In October 1908, Hitler tried again to gain entrance to the *Academy of Fine Arts*. He determinedly kept his dream alive. Living with a friend at the time, not even seeking work, he held out for that dream career as an artist. However, this time his paintings were judged so poorly he wasn't even allowed to take the actual exam. He began another final spiral to the bottom. He spent all of his savings, and then had to sell everything he owned. He ended up sleeping on park benches, begging for money, homeless, unshaven, dirty, wearing tattered clothes without even an overcoat.

Finally in December of 1909, freezing, half starved and broken mentally he moved into a homeless shelter. A few months later, he moved into a poor house for men where he would stay for the next few years. In a letter he wrote, *"I never knew the beautiful word* youth.*"* And this is definitely the case. In his mind, it seems he is destined to go from one tragedy to the next.

You can definitely feel the pain in Adolph's words. This is certainly a difficult situation for anyone to go through, but what really makes it unbearable is his view. Now you may be asking, "How on earth does anyone have a positive attitude in that situation?"

If a person's mental state is negative, they will see all of this as much more than just being hungry. And that's where the real pain lies. They see it as being worthless, unloved and cast out from God's grace. Notice his comments such as *"break them mercilessly in the end"*. You can feel his bitterness towards God and his fellowman oozing from his words. Think about how much different his attitude would have been had he somehow maintained a faithful relationship with his Creator throughout this situation. Yes, the physical suffering would have been there, but physical pain is much easier to deal with than spiritual pain. And fear is spiritual pain.

It is my firm feeling and understanding he's hurt and he's blaming his pain on the "horrible" things he went through. But that's not why he's in pain. By the time he wrote this book his "financially hard times" were over. So what's his point? His point is justification. Justification for the fearful view he believed to be reality. The reality he wanted others to see as well. He needed the rest of the world to see the monsters he saw. He needed the rest of the world to fight with him against these monsters. Because he was one thing…scared.

A FEARFUL VIEW SOLIDIFIES

Adolph goes on with more fearful justification using the "horror" of poverty, *"…the constant fluctuations thus caused by earnings and expenditure finally destroyed the sense of thrift for many people and also the habit of regulating expenditure in an intelligent way. The body appeared to grow accustomed to the vicissitudes of food and hunger, eating heartily in good times and going hungry in bad. Indeed hunger shatters all plans for rationing expenditure on a regular scale in better times when employment is again found. The reason for this is that the deprivations which the unemployed worker has to endure must be compensated for psychologically by a persistent mental mirage in which he imagines himself eating heartily once again. And this dream develops into such a longing that it turns into a morbid impulse to cast off all self-restraint when work and wages turn up again. Therefore the moment work is found anew he forgets to regulate the expenditures of his earnings but spends them to the full without thinking of to-morrow. … the earnings will last scarcely for a day; and finally they will disappear in one night of feasting.*

Often there are wife and children at home. And in many cases it happens that these become infected by such a way of living, especially if the husband is good to them and wants to do the best he can for them and loves them in his own way and according to his own lights."

Notice he uses poverty as a "warm up" fear. It's such a universal basic fear it lays a perfect foundation to build the rest of his fearful structure upon.

"…according to his own lights." I thought this was an interesting choice of words. It's as though he's saying according to what they feel inside is right, making reference to a good heart, or "God" heart inside of them.

Could that be the light of God he's referring to? Yet, despite his recognition of this, he's blinded by fear and confusion. One thing people will feel when they fear God is confusion, because the equation doesn't make sense. They will see in at least some people, good hearts, or God hearts. But the confusion comes in with all of the "bad" they see around them. They have to view God as "bad" in some way or themselves and other men as "bad". But where this doesn't make sense is how can God be bad if the beings He creates (at least some of them) are good? Can people be better than their Creator?

Hitler was stuck in the middle of an invalid equation leaving him scared, confused, insecure and bitter. I want to point out his good intentions in the situation DESPITE all of his fears. Notice the contrast of his good desires working against his fear. His concern is not just for himself, but I believe sincerely for others. He goes out of his way to give valid examples of how poverty affects a family, and I believe he sincerely wants to change this somehow. In fact, he is so determined to make a difference the rest of his life is committed to it. I believe deep inside he had a good heart with good intentions, but as they went through his foundational beliefs these good intentions became severely negatively charged, twisted and distorted.

Adolph continues on about the impoverished family example, *"The family eat and drink together as long as the money lasts and at the end of the week they hunger together."* (It's almost as if Hitler is saying, "This is what the so called 'loving' father got for following his 'own lights'") *"Then the wife wanders about furtively in the neighborhood, borrows a little and runs up small debts with the shopkeepers, in an effort to pull through the lean days towards the end of the week. They sit down together to the midday meal, with only meager fare on the table, and often even nothing to eat. They wait for the coming pay-day, talking of it and making plans; and while they are thus hungry they dream of the plenty that is to come. And so the little children become acquainted with misery in their early years.*

But the evil culminates when the husband goes his own way from the beginning of the week and the wife protests, simply out of love for the children. Then there are quarrels and bad feeling and the husband takes to drink according as he becomes estranged from his wife. He now becomes drunk every Saturday. Fighting for her own existence and that of the children, the wife has to hound him along the road from the factory to the tavern in order to get a few shillings from him on pay-day. Then when he finally comes home, maybe on the Sunday or the Monday, having parted with his last shillings and pence, pitiable scenes follow, scenes that cry out for God's mercy.

I have had actual experience of all this in hundreds of cases. At first I was disgusted and indignant; but later on I came to recognize the whole tragedy of their misfortune and to understand the profound causes of it. They were the unhappy victims of evil circumstances."

He actually paints a picture of perfect fear. He's absolutely right, this IS what happens when you give into fear. It does tear families apart. It does lead to hopelessness, poverty, addictions, etc.

GREED: A FEARFUL VIEW OF MONEY

Notice how he talks about how he is looking for the answer to this problem? At first he says he judged the individuals involved, saying he was disgusted and indignant at their behavior. But then a good thing happened when he realized he could actually understand how they got there and took the blame off them. However, here's where the problem lies for him. He says they were the unhappy victims of evil circumstances. Now truth be told, he's actually building a case against a specific group of people, but I want to point out the screwed up equation he's using. Originally he had his equation set as:

Evil People = Evil Situation

Based on his re-writing he came to:

Good People + Evil Situation = Misery

This is a fearful formula that causes Hitler then to search out who or what is responsible for this "Evil Situation". Because this is a fearful perspective, he doesn't realize this "Evil Situation" doesn't truly exist, not the way he's seeing it. He begins a mad search for the root of this problem with an insatiable desire to destroy it. I think of it like he's spinning the Wheel of Fear, even though no individual is responsible for the so-called "evil". Despite this, he's determined to find out who is. What he needed to see was the correct equation:

Good People + Faith through seemingly Hard Times = Eventual Prosperity

Because of Hitler's fear-based mentality, he saw life negatively. Sure, there are always people who appear to be going through hell. But if that's what you focus on, you'll be completely out of balance. The law of free agency says you always have the ability to see either positive or negative in your life, so you always have a true choice. No matter what I've gone through in my life, I had a choice to see it as positive or negative.

It's the classic story of the dog and his bone. There once was a dog who just obtained a bone, he loved the bone and is happily trotting home when he comes to a creek. As he looks into the water, he notices another dog with a bone. After a moment of thought, he makes the choice to open his mouth to grab the other bone, in the process dropping his own into the creek, where it's quickly whisked away downstream.

The typical moral of this story is the dog was "greedy" and because of his greed, he lost what he was blessed with. And though this is superficially true, it's still missing the core facts. Being "greedy" is another form of black and white mentality; it's another way of saying the dog had a "bad" trait within him called greed and because of the "bad greed" in him he was punished. And so applying this to ourselves it says, "Don't be 'bad' inside so bad things won't happen to you."

Do you see how virtually unhelpful this line of thinking is? It's like saying, "Okay, I'll stop being a 'bad' person. I was really excited to be bad, but now that you've told me this story I can see the error of my ways and I'll be 'good' inside from now on." This slight misunderstanding actually creates fear within us that if we are bad, then bad things will happen to us. Then when things happen that we see as bad, what happens? That's right; we're forced to see ourselves as bad!

But, this story is not about being bad or good, it's a story of...yes, you guessed it, Fear vs. Faith. The dog had everything he needed; the bone symbolizes his needs fulfilled. However, when the dog saw another bone his fear becomes evident. He had a fear that "There's not enough to go around. God doesn't give me everything I need, and so I have to take in order to survive. There's never any extra and maybe now for once I'll have a little extra, a little more security." And because the dog feared not having enough, he felt he needed to take the other bone as well. Notice his focus wasn't positive. Had it been a faithful view he would have focused on how blessed he was to have the bone and believed he'd always be blessed with bones as he needed them.

This would have allowed the natural love in his heart to flow and making him feel even that another one of his brothers had his needs filled as well.

Instead, his negative or fearful focus was on want and scarcity, even though he had his needs filled at that very moment! Pride or greed doesn't get any satisfaction out of having something, but only having more of it than someone else. Just the same, fear focuses not on what you have, but what you don't have.

As humans, we don't have some greed gene programmed within us that gives us the need to take from others, just because. In fact, the proof is all around us. Take men, for example. If men were inherently greedy, why would any man in his right mind get married? I mean, come on, if you're greedy it would mean you'd have to be really stupid at the same time. Because you just gave up 50% of your income! Yeah, Yeah, I know you may be thinking more like 100%, but I didn't want to be the one to say it. And women, if you were greedy you'd have to be insane to want to have children. By choosing to have children you effectively gave up 110% of everything; your time, energy, love, patience, and in some cases physical appearance!

No, I don't think the inherent greediness theory holds much water. However, I could easily make a case for the fact we have an innate desire to take care of one another. As a husband, I've found greater happiness in caring for my wife and children than in any other effort in my life. And I can speak for my wife as well, who I've watched truly give up everything for her marriage and children, and I have seen her happiness and purpose grow massively, despite the "sacrifice". And this is not something we had to force ourselves to want, it came naturally from inside.

Shortly after we were married, for my wife, the desire to have children came very, very naturally. It was like some evil witch doctor had implanted a "child craving disease". I mean we had to get a dog, (how many couples do that?) initially to curb her urges. It's like women walk around thinking, "m-m-must n-n-nurture!" Our three beautiful children have up to this point satisfied her craving. Now of course she walks around saying, "m-m-must g-g-get away from evil c-c-children".

So there's no way I'm going to accept we are greedy beings who need to be told not to be that way. And changing our programming or who we really are is a fear-based belief that will lead only to frustration.

Instead, understanding who we really are and overcoming fear and building faith is the secret to happiness in this life. It's what allows us to embrace our Creator, every other human being, and most of all, ourselves.

Hitler's view became completely negatively focused. All he saw was the "want" the "hard times" the "scarcity" the "evil". Just like any other time in the history of the world, we can focus on the negative, but I guarantee there was plenty of positive all around him he chose not to see. This was the height of the Industrial Revolution; amazing inventions were sprouting up all over the world, and scientific advances were occurring rapidly, especially in America. Freedom of religion was beginning to take hold around the world for the first time in human history!

He saw everything through the dark and dreary glasses of fear. And to someone who feels like they deserve a world that's awful, sometimes the only comfort they find is the validation of that belief. When we are scared we want the rest of the world to validate our fears. Look how scary it is! Please be scared with me! Help me fight these very real monsters!

We're all here to face our fears and come out with our faith strengthened. As Hitler displays, it didn't matter he was no longer in that "horrible" situation. He still felt the same way. Happiness and peace isn't a result of outside forces. Though he's trying hard to sell the fact that his issue was an external one, the true is that it was an internal one. The problem was in himself.

FEAR SUFFOCATES COMPASSION

This is such a great example of the power of fear and how it subtly works in our lives. Hitler continues on about his sentiments and impoverished experiences, *"I am thankful for that period of my life, because it hardened me and enabled me to be as tough as I now am. And I am even more thankful because I appreciate the fact that I was thus saved from the emptiness of a life of ease and that of a mother's darling was taken from tender arms and handed over to Adversity as to a new mother. Though I then rebelled against it as too hard a fate, I am grateful that I was thrown into a world of misery and poverty... ...In the case of such person hard struggle through which he passes often destroys his normal human sympathy. His own fight for existence kills his sensibility for the misery of those who have been left behind. ... Today I fervidly thank Providence for having sent me to such a school. ... In my own life similar hardships prevented me from giving way to a pitying sentimentality at the sight of these degraded products which had finally resulted from the pressure of circumstances. No, the sentimental attitude would be the wrong one to adopt. ...During my struggle for existence in Vienna I perceived very clearly that the end of all social activity must never be merely sentimental charity, which is ridiculous and useless, (but should be solved with) a ruthless determination to prune away all excrescence which are incapable of being improved.*

Speaking of the solution to this social problem of poverty he says, *"When the individual is no longer burdened with his own consciousness of blame in this regard, then and only then will he have the inner tranquility and outer force to cut off drastically and ruthlessly all the parasite growth and root out the weeds."*

Here is his rationalization for leaving his compassion and human sympathy behind. What he is saying is, "If God is going to treat me this awfully then I'm going to do the world a favor and prepare them for what God's really like."

Hitler goes on and on about how passionate and patriotic he is about forcing change in the country which he loves. I do believe he truly loved his country, and wanted to protect its citizens. But his foundational beliefs wouldn't allow him to carry these intentions out to a positive end. His deep seated fear forced him past normal boundaries most don't cross. Their faith will usually pull them "back from the ledge". But this would not happen for Adolph, his bitterness and anger would direct nearly every decision for the rest of his life.

Because fear is a void of faith, love, acceptance and worth; you can see his attempt to fill this void by his over-zealous patriotism. Whatever we feel inside is what will create the world outside. He was filled with bitterness and pain. And his actions brought our world some of the greatest bitterness and pain it's ever known.

Driven by this fear, he begins looking for the "culprit", who's responsible for everything that's bad in this world. This is not a new feeling. I've seen this in myself and others. We look for the "bad" in the world and seek to stamp it out. The problem is there are only people in this world. So where do we find the so-called "bad"? It has to be other people. This is why the core belief we are good is so important. When you fail to see that people are good, then it becomes ever so easy to interpret the acts of others as "evil-intended".

Once again, these fearful individuals tend to become conspiracy theorists. They are constantly looking for the "evil individual's" conspiracies, which they fear themselves to be the victim of.

SEARCHING FOR AN ANSWER TO HIS PAIN

Hitler's the epitome of a conspiracy theorist. It's not clear exactly when he finally came to the conclusion the Jews were "the ones to blame", the ones responsible for everything wrong with his life and country. But he mentions in his book that at first he blamed the German people themselves, having several bad experiences during his young working career. He seemed to have a difficult time forming friendships due to his intense feelings on nearly every topic, especially politics.

Adolph was so aggressive and confrontational that in one instance, his co-workers were so incensed by him they threatened to throw him off the construction scaffolding they stood on if he didn't leave. This turned out to be why he lost more than one job; simply because of his abrasive attitude towards others.

He talked about how bitter and angry he was after this event, speaking of these former co-workers, "...I asked myself: Are these men worthy of belonging to a great people? The question was profoundly disturbing; for if the answer were 'Yes', then the struggle to defend one's nationality is no longer worth all the trouble and sacrifice we demand of our best elements if it be in the interest of such a rabble. On the other hand, if the answer had to be 'No-these men are not worthy of the nation,' then our nation is poor *indeed in men. During those days of mental anguish and deep meditation I saw before my mind the ever increasing and menacing army of people who could no longer be reckoned as belonging to their own nation."*

Adolph is up to this point trying to build such a strong case about how hard it is to keep a job and survive; as if fate just wouldn't help him in anyway. Yet in this instance he had a job and lost it. He of course views himself the victim of evil circumstances, and so he misses the very cause, the negative source within him destroys each new thing that begins to grow in his life.

At this point, he's hinting the blame toward the Jewish people among others. Fear causes its host to become self-appointed judges of man. Naturally, if you can't trust men, or their good hearts, then someone needs to become the human police, determining who is good and who is bad. Again, this is not an abnormal feeling. Most of us feel this, to one degree or another, at some point in our lives, if not throughout most of our entire lives.

Hitler then begins looking into Social Democracy, which was becoming a big deal in Germany at the time. He abhorred the whole belief of it, and saw it as a brainwashing technique to dumb down the German people into submission of something awful.

"This probing into books and newspapers and studying the teaching of Social Democracy reawakened my love for my own people. And thus what at first seemed an impassable chasm became the occasion of a closer affection. Having once understood the working of the colossal system for poisoning the popular mind, only a fool could blame the victims of it. ...I am grateful for the ordeal which I had to go through at that time; for it was the means of bringing me to think kindly again of my own people, inasmuch as the experience enabled me to distinguish between the false leaders and the victims who have been led astray."

Here he turns back to his own people, and focuses his anger on a specific political party. Once again, not too unusual, even in our own country there can be extreme bitterness and fear between political divisions.

Then Hitler seeks to dial it down even further, still trying to find the root of all of his problems. *"In confronting the theoretical falsity and absurdity of the doctrine with the reality of its external manifestations, I gradually came to have a clear idea of the ends at which it aimed. During such moments I had dark presentiments and **feared** something **evil.** (big surprise, right?) I had before me a teaching inspired by egoism and hatred, mathematically calculated to win its victory, but the triumph of which would be a mortal blow to humanity. Meanwhile I had discovered the relations existing between this destructive teaching and the specific character of a people, who up to that time had been to me almost unknown. Knowledge of the Jews is the only key whereby one may understand the inner nature and therefore the real aims of Social*

Democracy."

Okay, are you a little freaked out by that? You naturally should be because that's its purpose. It's fear, and it's contagious. But we are NOT going to fear it; instead we'll see it for what it is.

So now he's "feared something evil". Yes, we're getting the picture. To him this was all real. It was his belief, which made it his reality. From his fearful perspective, he sincerely does believe these people to be evil. He begins to wield his power of creation through belief.

He goes on to clarifies the fact that he didn't always feel that way. *"I will not say that the manner in which I first became acquainted with it was particularly unpleasant for me. In the Jew I still saw only a man who was of a different religion, and therefore, on grounds of human tolerance, I was against the idea that he should be attacked because he had a different faith. And so I considered that the tone adopted by the anti-Semitic Press in Vienna was unworthy of the cultural traditions of a great people. The memory of certain events which happened in the Middle Ages came into my mind, and I felt that I should not like to see them repeated. Generally speaking, these anti-Semitic newspapers did not belong to the first rank but I did not then understand the reason of this---and so I regarded them more as the product of jealousy and envy rather than the expression of a sincere, though wrong-headed, feeling. My own opinions were confirmed by what I considered to be the infinitely more dignified manner in which the really great Press replied to those attacks or simply ignored them, which later seemed to me the most respectable way.*

It's ironic he even says the anti-Jewish papers seemed low class at first to him, a product of jealousy and envy. He also thought the way the Great Press, which was the Jewish Press, replied by ignoring it was the "most respectable way". Yes, I'm with you; he should have stuck with this first impression. And now Hitler begins to see the evil in the *Great Vienna Press* which in other words to him was the "Great Jewish Press".

He writes, *"And at the time these newspapers took up an attitude of anxiety in matters that concerned the German Emperor, trying to cloak their enmity by the serious air they gave themselves. But in my eyes that enmity appeared to be only poorly cloaked. Naturally they protested that they had no intention of mixing in Germany's internal affairs-God forbid! They pretended that by touching a delicate spot in such a friendly way they were fulfilling a duty that devolved upon them by reason of the mutual alliance between the two countries and at the same time discharging their obligations of journalistic truthfulness. Having thus excused themselves about tenderly touching a sore spot, they bored with the finger ruthlessly into the wound. That sort of thing made my blood boil. And now I began to be more and more on my guard when reading the great Vienna Press.*

So here he obviously is saying he blames the press, the same press he previously respected he now loathed as he sees the Jews behind it. Notice the same feeling coming from him over the press as he expressed about the wealthy, which coincidently in his mind were Jewish as well.

"My ideas about anti-Semitism (anti-Jew) *changed over the course of time, but that was the change which I found most difficult. It cost me a greater internal conflict with myself, and it was only after a struggle between reason and sentiment that victory began to be decided in favor of the former. Two years later sentiment rallied to the side of reason and became a faithful guardian and counselor."*

Just to interpret a little, he's saying he struggled between reason and sentiment, meaning his "reasoning" was these people were destructive to the stability of Germany, so they must be disposed of. His sentiment is his morality or what I call his "inner goodness" pulling against him telling him that's not right. Yes I know, thanks, Hitler, for mentioning it. But this so called "reason" was actually nothing more than fear at its ugliest. So he put it very well, his fear drowned out his inner God which told him it wasn't right. He also justifies that two years later when "sentiment" rallied to the side of reason and became a faithful guardian and counselor. Here we see how ugly the monster of fear can be as he claims that sentiment was now with him justifying his fear. This is obviously bull. Sentiment was no longer a luxury his fear could afford. Fear was speaking for sentiment who was now buried in the back yard.

His morals and rationale now vanishing; he began acting out on his horrific fear. From the early 1920s to the early 1930s, Hitler began entrenching these fears on an already fearful public who had just been shamed by the rest of the world for their WWI embarrassment. He did this by generating attention through fearful propaganda, his book, and public rallies. Fear begets more fear, and a ripe public began accepting him, until he was elected Chancellor of Germany in 1933.

I want to point out how much more effort negative fearful energy takes. Just as it takes more muscles to frown than to smile, it takes significantly more work to lie than to tell the truth. Fear leads to exhausting efforts of energy to justify and validate it. Just as he mentions in his own words, morally he knew it wasn't right, so he goes to massive effort to justify it. You'll see how he had to search and search for some way he could justify his fears and feel "right" about doing what his heart told him was wrong.

He continues by saying, *"At the time of this bitter inner struggle, between calm* reason (he's calling his irrational fear calm reason) *and the sentiments in which I had been brought up,* (meaning he was taught morality and human rights) *the lessons that I learned on the streets of Vienna rendered me invaluable assistance* (meaning the awful hard times he went through strengthened his fear to the point he could justify going against his former morality) *A time came when I no longer passed blindly along the streets of the mighty city, as I had done in earlier days,* (meaning before I was ignorant because I didn't know about how "bad" the world really was) *but now with my eyes open not only to study the buildings but also the human beings* (I now know there are evil people all around and I will now find them as the self-appointed judge).

Once, when passing through the Inner City, I suddenly encountered a phenomenon in a long caftan (a full length cloak*) and wearing black sidelocks. My first thought was: Is this a Jew? They certainly did not have the appearance in Linz. I watched the man stealthily and cautiously; but the longer I gazed at that strange countenance and examined it feature by feature, the more the question shaped itself in my brain: Is this a German?"*

What he's really hinting at here is—is this a human being? We're looking at the ultimate goal of fear, to get man to turn against man, brother against brother. Here he is, of course, selling this to the German people to get them to buy a ticket on the Hitler train of fear.

And now here comes more of his fear-based rationalizations, it's almost comical at how hard he has to try to make them look inhumane so justification can be found for his ultimate fear-driven goal.

He continues on, *"Naturally I could no longer doubt that here there was not a question of Germans who happened to be of a different religion but rather that there was a question of an entirely different people. For as soon as I began to investigate the matter and observe the Jews, then Vienna appeared to me in a different light."*... (Meaning now that he looked through the eyes of fear, he sees darkness) *"Wherever I now went I saw Jews, and the more I saw of them the more strikingly and clearly they stood out as a different people from the other citizens. ...in outer appearance (they) bore no similarity to Germans."*

Interesting, before he had this fear of them, he said he never noticed them, but now they stick out like sore thumbs and they look nothing like Germans. You can see fear is not based on reality; remember it's always based on something non-existent. So he has to go out of his way to try to create this case, which is the goal, to prove the Jews are so far removed from the Germans that he can justify getting rid of them.

One thing that really scared Hitler at this point is he felt like the Jews had such a stronghold on Germany. Apparently there was a splinter group of Jews that started a movement called Zionism which supposedly had the purpose of asserting Judaism on the national character of Austria and Germany. And his fear fed anger of them continued to increase. You can see how hard he is now stretching to demean these people in his following words.

"Cleanliness, whether moral or of another kind, had its own peculiar meaning for these people. That they were water-shy was obvious on looking at them and, unfortunately, very often also when not looking at them at all. The odor of those people in caftans often used to make me feel ill. Beyond that there were the unkempt clothes and ignoble exterior. All these details were certainly not attractive; but the revolting feature was that beneath their unclean exterior one suddenly perceived the moral mildew of the chosen race."

Honestly, I hate even quoting these words. The reason I feel I can is because I see them for what they are; complete nonsense and the ranting of fear-fueled insanity. But it's necessary to hear in order to see fear for what it really is and what it really can become. This last statement is not based on any reality whatsoever. I want to point out how silly and ridiculous his statements become.

I also feel it's really important to point out his last three words, *"the chosen race"*. All along we've felt his subtle anger and bitterness towards God, the God that took everything from him, and the God that wouldn't help his father, wouldn't save his brother or his mother and wouldn't help him in any area of his life. Now he comes across a group of people who claim they are the "chosen people" of God. Because of his deep-seated fear towards God these people, who stand as witnesses of faith in the love of God, are too much for him.

To him they stood as witnesses of his worthlessness simply because they believed they were of worth. I can hear him saying, "How DARE you believe you're loved when I've never allowed myself to believe that? How DARE you believe God takes care of you when my soul has cried out for help all my life!"

He's accusing the Jewish people of being the "mildew" of the "holy" Aryan race! Again to point out the lunacy, Hitler, most likely being a descendant of a Jew, had to be speaking of himself at the same time.

As a side note, another sign of the fear residing in Hitler's heart is the fact that multiple witnesses of Hitler describe his personality to be hysterical, meaning he was subject to frequent bouts of hysteria when things didn't go according to his plans. Anger and impatience are key symptoms of fear, just as peace and patience are key symptoms of faith.

More of his irrational banter, *"What soon gave me cause for very serious consideration were the activities of the Jews in certain branches of life, into the mystery of which I penetrated little by little. Was there any shady undertaking, any form of foulness, especially in cultural life, in which at least one Jew did not participate? On putting the probing knife carefully to that kind of abscess on immediately discovered, like a maggot in a putrescent body, a little Jew who was often blinded by the sudden light."*

Like I said, completely irrational, and it's so preposterous I couldn't help but laugh as I read it. He's really trying hard to prove how "bad" these Jews are. Notice how he needs to make sure he includes the entire race, which is completely black and white mentality. Fear drives him toward that all-or-nothing end.

Because fear is simply a perspective, we can easily find whatever we are searching for. If I look for the "bad" in people with my "fear-goggles" on, I see myself surrounded by them. And vise versa for faith.

He honestly believes he's finally found the source of all his misery and pain. The reality is the only person responsible for it was himself. He held the power within himself to solve his own suffering all along. It stands as proof, even after he had "extinguished" a massive chunk of this "evil" he felt no differently. It didn't bring him or his country the peace and happiness he'd promised.

Obviously he couldn't see what was really going on; he didn't see or understand the solution within himself. He had no clue where the path to peace for him was. So being blinded he would never find the true solution. In this situation we are so blessed because of the knowledge we now have about what led to this point in order to manage our own fears.

Here Hitler displays his fear of the Jews as if they are taking over the world and destroying it. *"In my eyes the charge against Judaism became a grave one the moment I discovered the Jewish activities in the Press, in art, in literature and the theater. All unctuous protests were now more or less futile. One needed only to look at the posters announcing the hideous productions of the cinema and theater, and study the names of the authors who were highly lauded there in order to become permanently adamant on Jewish questions."*

Can you say freak-out? And now that he's made the point that they're into everything, controlling everything, he makes the following point about their "evil" intentions"

"Here was a pestilence, a moral pestilence, with which the public was being infected. It was worse than the Black Plague of long ago. And in what mighty doses this poison was manufactured and distributed. Naturally the lower the moral and intellectual level of such an author of artistic products, the more inexhaustible his fecundity (rapid growth). *Sometimes it went so far that one of these fellows, acting like a sewage pump, would shoot his filth directly in the face of other members of the human race. In this connection we must remember there is no limit to the number of such people. ...Nature may bring into existence ten thousand such despoilers who act as the worst kind of germ-carriers in poisoning human souls. It was a terrible thought, and yet it could not be avoided, that the greater number of the Jews seemed specially destined by Nature to play this shameful part. And is it for this reason that they can be called the chosen people? ...*

Here again the life which I observed on the streets taught me what evil really is. ... I was happy at last to know for certain that the Jew is not a German. Thus I finally discovered who were the evil spirits leading our people astray."

Fear has taken Hitler to the point of no return; here are the steps:

1. Get Hitler to fear himself, creating an inexhaustible source of inner pain and conflict
2. Get Hitler to see the source of his pain as another human being or group of human beings, making those individuals evil and responsible
3. Make the fear of these people great enough to override his inner moral light
4. Propagate these fears to everyone with whom he has influence

Hitler crosses that fateful line of allowing himself to give into his fears, break through the foundational moral barriers of faith, and call another human being evil; thereby justifying the ultimate act of fear to separate and destroy man.

HIS FEAR SUPPORTED

He goes on and on in his book, taking great exhausting effort to prove his case against the Jews. One key piece he needed to help him cement his justification was found in the teachings of a man named Dr. Jorg Lanz Van Liebenfels, who was a defrocked monk (stripped of title and position). Liebenfels wrote a book in 1904 entitle *Theozoologie* in which he taught the theory of the Aryan race, which is the belief that God created a race of people who were superior in every way to others. They were referred to as Gottmenschen (god men) and these were the fair-skinned beings he warned should never intermix with dark-skinned lower races so their blood would remain pure and achieve their ultimate divinity by again ruling over the "dark-skinned beastmen". This included Semitic peoples as a lower race of people, just the fuel Adolph was looking for at the time.

This new information filled two needs for Hitler. The first is that it was a type of religion he could hold onto that said he was "better" than others especially the Jews. Finally, he found some type of band-aid to put over the hole in his heart. However, he eventually finds this does little to stop the pain. Secondly, it justified why it was actually okay to rid the world of these "evil" beings.

It's important to re-establish the fact that fear is a negative energy and people are the conductors of energy. In this case he was also the product of other's fears. Men he looked up to shaped his feelings and attitude. One man he highly regarded was a high school history teacher named Dr. Leopold Potsch, who taught him German History and instilled his undying devotion and commitment to Germany.

Another man who affected Hitler during his young adulthood was the mayor of Vienna and a noted anti-Semite, Karl Lueger. Hitler admired this man for his talents in speech and use of propaganda to sway public opinion. He even noted Lueger's skills in manipulating institutions such as the Catholic Church and assumed it as another tactic he would use later in life as a dictator.

So this is not just something Hitler came up with on his own. It was a tide of fear that was rising. Different men were spreading their seeds of fear and Hitler just happened to be a perfect host for the virus.

HITLER'S FIRST WAR: ANOTHER FAILURE

In 1913, Hitler finally moved to the "Great Motherland"—Germany—and settled in Munich. He got by, selling paintings of local landmarks to mainly Jewish shop owners.

In 1914 Hitler's dream came true when Germany declared war in World War I. When he first heard news of it he sank to his knees and thanked heaven he was alive. He eagerly enlisted as all his childhood fantasies of war and heroism played out in his mind. It's interesting to note the first event he actually viewed as good began to change his life. His determination and courage was displayed in this war, and even though he didn't make a great impression on his comrades who thought he was overzealous, higher authorities saw his spirit and he actually earned five medals of Honor for his service. One was the Iron Cross first class; which he earned because a Jew recommended him for it.

Why was war his great dream? Why would war be the one thing that made him grateful to be alive?! Imagine being scared your entire life. What's the one and only thing that's going to feel good? Fighting…fighting feels good when you're scared. It's validating and satiating because it feels like maybe you're killing some of the things you're afraid of. What are the natural autonomic responses to fear? Freeze, flight or fight.

In 1916, Hitler was injured by a shell fragment in his leg, which took him out of active service for a time. During this period, he became appalled at the apathy citizens showed towards the war. Hitler blamed the Jews for this and saw them as conspiring against the German war effort. What's really happening is they weren't as scared as he was. This made him extremely uncomfortable.

As the tide of the war began to turn against Germany, Hitler became extremely depressed and would spend hours sitting in the corner of his tent, quietly contemplating, and then burst into a fit of rage, spouting it was the invisible forces of the Jews causing their defeat.

Hitler, finally making it back to the front lines, was again injured, temporarily blinded by chlorine gas. A month later he heard the news, Germany had lost the war. His cherished "Motherland" was no longer a monarchy but now a republic. Hitler describes his reaction, *"There followed terrible days and even worse nights – I knew that all was lost...in these nights hatred grew in me, hatred for those responsible for this deed."*

At this point, Hitler took all of the "awful" things that happened to him in his life, and though I believe he blamed God in his heart, he took it out on "God's People". He was bitter over everything; he mentions several times in bitterness the words "chosen people".

What he didn't realize, was he was a chosen person as well. All people are God's people if they choose to believe it. Adolph did not see himself as God's son, and so he had to take that right for himself. He would forcibly prove he was the chosen race by forcing the current chosen race into extinction. He loved the Aryan theory because it made him feel good about who he was. But it was based on a massive falsehood. The falsehood that we are not all chosen people, God's people, every race, sex, religion and creed; this IS a foundational principle of faith; the simple ignorance of which caused a negative impact to this world like no other.

Hitler did not understand the true source of his pain and did not realize he himself held the keys to unlock it. His book "My Struggle" is basically his story of his two wolves fighting for control. The end result is he fed the wolf of fear and permitted the wolf of faith to starve.

I want to give one more final quote about his view towards the Jews, not to overly discuss it, but it's important to see how he thought so we can recognize and eliminate the fears each of us struggle with. *"...it must be admitted that the original authors of this evil which has infected the nations were Devils incarnate. For only the brain of a monster, and not that of a man, could the plan of this organization take shape whose workings must finally bring about the collapse of human civilization and turn this world into a desert waste. Such being the case the only alternative left was to fight, and in that fight to employ all the weapons which the human spirit and intellect and will could furnish, leaving it to Fate to decide in whose favor the balance should fall."*

This is the final step of fearful progression. Notice he HAS to justify his enemies are "Devils incarnate", which means he is saying they ARE evil itself, in human form. It's a statement that they are NOT the offspring of God but of the Devil. Can you see the conflict he is going through? He can't justify killing another human being, the God within won't allow it, even as hard as he's tried to bury it. Instead, there is only one way a human can justify hurting another and that is to be blinded by fear. He, in his fearful mind, has justified they are NOT God's children, not created from the same source he was. His preprogrammed goodness won't allow him to do it, even despite his fear. He HAS to justify they are literally spawned of a Satan, so he can justify it to himself and to his fellow people.

Here are his words confirming this, *"Should the Jew…triumph over the people of this world, his Crown will be the funeral wreath of mankind, and this planet will once again follow its orbit through ether, without any human life on its surface, as it did millions of years ago. And so I believe to-day that my conduct is in accordance with the will of the Almighty Creator. In standing guard against the Jew I am defending the handiwork of the Lord."*

I've thought much about how to communicate my feelings as I've studied this man. Most of all, how did he come to this point, what happened to get him to perform such atrocities and how can we learn from this experience, how can we avoid that same result?

I believe that God exists and He is good. Secondly, we are His creations, making us good as well. We are connected to Him and each other, and anytime we feel any conflicting belief to those two beliefs then the conflicting belief is based in falsehood.

I believe we must have a love for ourselves in order to love others. Recognizing we are a creation of God's, created by love, and that to love ourselves is only to love what God created. Since we are all connected, it is impossible to hate ourselves and love our brother. The only time we feel negatively about ourselves is when we fear ourselves.

I've learned I don't have to be afraid of who I am. And because it isn't a question anymore, it's not a test I'm trying to pass. I am God's son. An integral part of God's human family, and so are you. Period. And I don't have to be afraid of who I am because inside I am good, and though I may be ignorant and mortal, at my core I am good.

I believe that Creator has already "saved" mankind, or in other words placed us in a position where we could never be lost. That principle is a key. Most religions believe this to one extent or another though they may call this principle of salvation by different names and sources. And what we call it really doesn't matter. What matters is that we believe it. Whether Buddha, Christ,

Krishna, Allah, God, Higher Power etc., the reality is that we're all created by the same source. And he is NOT a failure, which means neither are we.

It is this belief that allows me NOT to fear Hitler. Instead, I see him as an individual the same as me. God is always in charge despite what we can and will do to one another in fear. I know he has all things within his control and we are truly "saved", or in other words safe. There is nothing to fear.

THE PATH OF FEAR

Here is the path of fear I see Adolph taking. Hitler saw himself as the son of an illegitimate man; and even worse, his father most likely being the son of a Jew! I believe he resented and blamed the Jews for his illegitimacy. Notice how powerfully negative a fear-like bloodline can be. Faith says we are all connected, one God-family. There is no such thing as worth or lack of worth based on bloodline. What matters is what we believe. We are who we believe we are, either free-creators or slaves and prisoners. We are either victims or victors.

Hitler resented the loss of his mother because he saw it as another sign of his unworthiness of love. God took her from me because I obviously am unworthy of her. This is why he was so embittered by her death. He then turned his anger to her Jewish doctor, blaming him for her death. He no doubt resented the loss of his brother Edmund, and the fact that he had no real close ties to other family members. He felt cut off from love, when the reality is he cut himself off from it. Because of the false beliefs in his head, he would never allow himself to be committed in a loving relationship until the day before he took his life. He was much too scared to ever risk the pain of losing love, much too scared he wasn't worthy of it.

His failure to get into the Academy was devastating to him because he allowed it to be more negative validation he was not "good enough". He gave into his fears and let it take him to the bottom, a homeless beggar. The resulting effects of fear were the destruction of everything he had, but most importantly the destruction of himself. I believe he blamed God as he saw this as another sign of his inner worthlessness. Seeing the wealthy "chosen people of God" was what he believed to be validation of his own fear, especially during this time of poverty. They became the symbol of all of his fears and thus the target of evil.

However, despite being on the bottom, he was blessed to be completely saved from it. Yes here's a man complaining about how life sucks because of how little he had, but nothing changed in him when he came into full control of one of the largest empires in the world. He was one of the wealthiest men on the planet at the time, but it did nothing to change his feelings. The external things of the world never do and never can. Our world exists in our mind and heart. It's here where we define it, whether it be an awful place of fear, or a beautiful place of faith.

He saw the war as his dream come true. But the failure of it—another devastating blow. Like a judge's gavel declaring the failure of every dream of his life.

THROUGH THE EYES OF FAITH

Let's think about the complete falsity of fear for a moment. You can see very clearly how Hitler came to the ridiculous conclusion that the Jews were responsible for everything wrong in his life, but if you turn this around and view it through the eyes of faith the picture changes completely.

- If it was truly a Jewish boy who impregnated his grandmother, then it was a Jew that gave him life!
- If he believed they were a chosen people, then so was he!
- The Jewish doctor he blamed for the loss of his mother was in fact the only person TRYING TO SAVE HIS MOTHER'S LIFE!
- It was mainly Jewish shop owners that bought his paintings during his years of poverty. Had it not been for them, he would have starved.
- One of his proudest achievements, the Iron Cross, was achieved because of the recommendation of a Jew.

These are VERY surface observations I've made from just a little bit of information. I'm sure if we had more information on his connectedness with the Jews, there would be volumes of evidence to support how important they were in his life. When you look at how connected we are as men and women, you can see as Hitler was annihilating the Jewish people, he was very much annihilating himself, he was destroying the organism he was an integral part of, and eventually end it by taking his own life.

As you're well aware, Hitler in his reign as Fuhrer, acted out all of his fears. He harnessed the power of destruction and used it to a devastating effect upon mankind and himself. He started the bloodiest campaign in the history of the modern world, in which millions upon millions lost their lives. To this very day, we feel the effects of the fear of this one man. To say we are not all connected is to ignore the pain we feel when we view this part of human history.

Not only did Hitler destroy millions of lives, but his fear and paranoia caused him to take the lives of his own men. He saw God as cruel to him and so he believed that's who he should be as well. He made the following statement cited in *Joachim Fest's* 1975, *"Nature is cruel; therefore we are also entitled to be cruel. When I send the flower of German youth into the steel hail of the next war without feeling the slightest regret over the precious German blood that is being spilled, should I not also have the right to eliminate millions of an inferior race that multiplies like vermin?"*

God is not cruel, God is good, but what we believe becomes our reality. For Hitler, he saw God as cruel and so Hitler created a cruel world, what he feared became his reality until the bitter end.

Hitler's path of fear went on and on, he eventually cut out all his military generals and took over direct control of his troops, he could trust no one, not even his so-called German brothers, his fellow Aryan people. And because he believed he could trust no one, that's exactly what happened. Some of his own leaders plotted his assassination, seeing him for the mad man he truly was. He thwarted numerous plots, and then watched films of their punishment by death; feeling like the only security and control he had in life was the security and control he created by his fear and paranoia.

In late April 1945, as the Russian troops marched toward the capital of Germany and defeat became emanate, Hitler gave his last orders that whatever was left of Germany should be destroyed--manufacturing, communications and transportation. He was determined if he couldn't have it, no one would. In other words, if he didn't deserve, no one else should. He had to force equality because he couldn't see it already existed.

It is not ironic but a matter of natural law, Hitler's greatest fear was the destruction of the great Germany. **What we fear, we create.** Remember, fear is faith going in the wrong direction. By fearing it, he believed it. His fear of losing everything he loved was simply a belief he was going to lose everything he loved. He believed it and believed it and believed it, until by his amazing creative power of faith it became real.

It existed first as a reality in the world of his mind. This is the world of creation where all physical things are born. He created the ultimate culmination of his fears. And Germany was destroyed like no other country before or since.

Hitler's love for the country was real. But remember it is not whether we love or don't love that determines our reality; it is what we believe that determines our reality. And so despite his love for the people, art, culture, architecture, literature, industry, science and even the landscape, it was, in at least in part, destroyed.

Imagine if he could have seen the truth that his fears were completely non-existent. Think about it, what did he really want? He wanted to be accepted of Germany and its culture, its landscape, its people. What was keeping him from it? He had it right there in his hands! Just like the dog with the bone, but fear of losing it caused that exact result.

This lesson is a great one for me. Many times I've thought in frustration, why can't I JUST BE HAPPY?! I have to stop myself and think, what "happiness ingredients" am I missing? NOTHING! I'm not missing anything I need to be happy; it's all right in front of me. But in every case where I'm robed of peace and security it is due to fear.

It makes me think of how silly my fears can be. The day I was married to the love of my life was absolutely amazing; I was so overwhelmed by gratitude and joy. That night we slept in a beautiful hotel suite and the next day we got up to catch a plane to Florida for our honeymoon. But guess what? I was already unhappy again! The very day after the greatest day of my life, I was back to my old unhappy place! Uuuggghhhh, fear can be so exhausting. My new bride was concerned and I didn't really have any explanations; but the truth was - I was scared. I swear if there is something to be scared of I could find it. And can you guess what my fear was now? Not too different from Hitler's I have to admit. I was scared it was too good to be true; I was scared that somehow I was going to lose her.

When I look hard at myself, I realize my fear says I'm "unworthy" of good things; because deep inside I'm not good, at least not completely good. There are "bad" things about me and therefore if something really good comes into my life I can't accept it. It can't have the desired effect to bring happiness because how can you be happy about having something you don't believe you deserve? On the outside, this would look like simple ingratitude, but that is just a superficial symptom this deeper fear. As with my wife, since I didn't feel worthy of her, I believed justice would balance things out and somehow I would lose her. This is a very natural feeling, but if fed too long begins to erode the good in our life. If I held that fearful belief long enough I'd create the reality of not having her.

In contrast, I've worked at cultivating the belief God is Good, and heaven knows we've got enough proof all around us. Even Hitler would have to admit (in his faithful state of mind) we live in a beautiful world. He was blessed with a loving mother, and a father who, despite his fear, had good intentions for him. He was blessed with wonderful talents to paint and speak, and had he been able to see it, would have found himself surrounded by good, loving people, many of which were Jewish.

He would have seen that despite his radical actions to separate and protect himself from others, thus insulating himself from love, he was blessed with a loving companion in Eva Braun. A beautiful woman, who was so committed in her love to him, she stayed with him to the very bitter end. He finally married her just days before they together took their lives.

He was too scared he wasn't worthy of her devotion, and only married her when he sensed the end was upon them. Was this not what he was looking for? And was not everything he needed to be happy, right there in front of him?

On April 30, 1945, when Russian troops were literally two blocks from the Reich Chancellery, Hitler stood dazed and confused at the fact all of his fearful plans had failed. And, I believe there was a part of him, buried deep inside, that was relieved, relieved that maybe, just maybe, he was wrong. If you spent your life in an awful hellish world you felt you had no other choice but to accept as real, you'd have to feel at least some relief if you found you were wrong.

And so he met the fate he'd always feared, he was hated and despised at this point by the entire world. So he put a gun to his mouth while biting on a cyanide capsule. Eva Braun took her life as well, and they were taken by their aides, their bodies burned as the Russian troops stormed the capital.

It's important to recognize another point about Hitler. Since we tend to view him as "evil", I think it's important to realize as far as my studies go, Hitler never broke the law except in two cases. The first was he dodged the Austrian draft, then later when caught, he wrote a letter of apology in which he related the trials of his life in such a way the officer in charge actually felt sympathetic toward Adolph and forgave him of the crime. The second incident was when Hitler took part in a political demonstration that got him incarcerated for about a year. Other than this, despite the poverty and trials of his life, he never broke the law that I could find. This man we tend to see as inherently evil did not start out his life running around like a madman killing, steeling, raping etc.

Of course all of these things and worse were acted out under his reign, but he was technically, legally accepted into power. He was very upfront about what he thought needed to be done for their country. The people, in part, had similar fears, which made them a match energetically. Hitler waved the flag of fear and many responded in like. This was further validation to him that what he believed really WAS real. This only cemented his determination. Had there not been the same fear of Jews to some extent among the people, he would have been powerless. No one can control us using fear if we aren't afraid. However, as long as there is fear within us, it will act as a steering wheel with which anyone with the same fear can freely control us.

Again, understanding this is not justification for the awful negative results, but the very opposite; to truly see what caused those negative results. Because to write off the situation as, "Well we don't really understand what the heck happened with Adolph, it must have been the evil virus; let's hope we don't catch it. We'll just keep our guns loaded and ready for the next individual that shows any signs of it." Give us no power or understanding about the truth and it doesn't stop the insanity. It simply spreads the same fear and his reign of fear lives on.

Seeing through the power of faith, and understanding the force of fear, is the only way to ever come to a true answer as to what "right" really is. With fear in the mix, "right" becomes subjective to the fears of the individual. Killing becomes "right" if you're scared enough. So despite the awful negative, we see Hitler had the capacity to love, and we see even more his desire to be loved. Last of all, we saw he was loved, dearly by his mother, by his father and by Eva who, as difficult as it may be to understand, saw something in him that allowed her to love him.

UNDERSTANDING BRINGS PEACE

So how do we deal with this knowledge, and how should we feel towards Hitler and his reign of terror? I read an article from *Time Magazine* highlighting the top 100 most influential people in the world written in 1998. I believe it typifies the feelings of many people.

The author subtitles the story as, *"The avatar of fascism posed the century's greatest threat to democracy and redefined the meaning of evil forever".* The article starts by reading, *"I take on this essay with fear and trembling. That's because although defeated, although dead, this man is frightening."* I'll give you a few more highlights I picked out of the article to give you a feel for my point.

"Adolph Hitler or the incarnation of absolute evil... ...the Satan and exterminating angel feared and hated by all others... Even today, works on his enigmatic personality and his cursed career are bestsellers everywhere. ...all seem to respond to an authentic curiosity on the part of the public haunted by memory and the desire to understand. ... But when later we evoke the 20th century, among the first names that will surge to mind will be that of a fanatic with a mustache who thought to reign by selling the soul of his people to the thousand demons of hate and of death."

This article was very well-written, and I believe typifies general feelings towards Hitler because we're all going to feel scared of him. But let's think through the results of such feelings. We fear him because we don't understand him or how he could do what he did. We tend to think of him the very same way he thought of the Jews. Notice we are calling him the VERY SAME names he used to label the Jews. We are saying he truly is separate from "us". We are good, he is evil, and thus the justification for taking lives goes around the boundaries of morality again.

Now we might think that's easy to justify, he clearly killed millions of innocent people and the Jews didn't, so that makes him wrong and us right. But this is actually missing the point. The point is the only problem we as mankind have is to fear one another. By this very belief, we step onto a sandy foundation, because if Hitler, who we cannot deny is a member of mankind, our own relative, is truly evil and only capable of evil, then we open Pandora's Box. Who else then is evil? And the fearful hunt begins. Don't misinterpret fearing Hitler as understanding him. Nothing is learned or gained wearing the blindfold of fear. It's the same one he wore on his journey into darkness.

I'm not saying he shouldn't have been stopped. Of course he had to be stopped. When we work against the natural laws of the universe it will always step in to correct our false theories. But understanding and stopping the cycle is much different than striking back in ignorant fear. To do so is to drink the same poison that caused the insanity.

Fear impairs our ability to learn anything from him. Just as Hitler learned the hard way, what you fear most, you bring about. So it is with us. By fearing him, we create another cycle of fear. Fear breeds fear. The fear of suffering breeds suffering. If we want to heal from the past of Hitler, we let go of our fear of him and realize from a standpoint of truth and understanding, we have nothing to fear.

Fear being negative energy and we being conductors of energy naturally tend to conduct the negative energy from this situation. Just reading about the atrocities of Hitler's reign fills us with negative energy. That's because it WAS negative. We instantly feel it the second we touch it, but we must become proactively positive conductors. We must neutralize the negative energy and then translate it into positive energy. Why? Because if we don't, if we accept that negative energy it will contaminate us, just as it did millions of people back then and millions today. You'll begin to feel its destructive effects in your soul, as you harbor the fruits of fear which are anger, bitterness and the need for revenge. You'll transfer this negative energy, at least on this subject, to individuals whom you come in contact with, infecting them with the same corrosive energy.

If you believe Hitler to be your enemy, then this is your reality and you'll begin immediately to feel him hurt you even today, decades later. Your pain will be very real, but based on the falsehood of fear. Thus if Hitler is your enemy and if his intentions were to destroy the hope of mankind, then you are right and he continues to win wars within your heart.

As Dr. Wayne Dyer explains in his incredible book *The Power of Intention*, *"There is no amount of pain you can feel that will make one person feel better."* Pain begets pain. Suffering begets suffering. Fear begets fear. Anger begets anger.

No, fearing Hitler is NOT the answer. Fear is the power of destruction no matter the justification. Even if we think we're using it for "good", the resulting effect will not be goodness. Like we sometimes refer to as "selling our soul to the Devil'; using fear to accomplish "good" never succeeds except in creating more fear.

Fearing him is like the child who touches the hot stove and fears touching anything else remotely close to it. We then will have to fear others around us, especially those in power, we'll scrutinize individuals looking for the Devil in them and driving ourselves crazy. Most of all, we allow negative energy to direct our lives; it inhibits our ability to love and feel love and our capacity to feel peace. It also slows our learning, growth and progression, thus keeping us in a state of damnation.

Looking back over history, fear has always been the cause for war. Take the English verses the American Indian. I could go on and on about how tens of thousands were killed over nothing more than illusions of fear. The Indians feared the white man coming to take their home. The white man feared the "savage" Indian destroying them. And now all it takes is the smallest validation of that fear, and boom, you have a war. Some of which were over the silliest of miscommunications, resulting in the loss of many lives.

So let's take it to the other extreme, should we pity Hitler? No, because pity is another form of negative energy. Pity is just another way of saying Hitler was just a "bad" person we're glad we aren't like. This still doesn't free us. It still allows negativity to breed from it. Pity validates fear in that it says, "Yes that really WAS a terrible situation." Which is like going up to someone who doesn't have sight, and saying, "Wow, you should be really, really unhappy because you don't have eyesight." Pity only validates the negative; it doesn't neutralize it.

Faith sees all things as good. It sees all people as good or "God-like". Faith is the only positive energy to neutralize the negative energy created by this event. The fruits of faith are forgiveness, understanding, love, positive action, compassion, and agency. Through faith, I have been able to see Adolph Hitler as my brother, one who came from the same source of good, which means he IS good or at least capable of good when in a positive state. However much like me and all men, his natural inclination to conduct negative energy was never balanced out. I am much like him in that I fear myself. It's a feeling we can all relate to. The eyes of faith see that there can be real healing from this event, real forgiveness, real growth.

My only desire for Hitler would be to show him, thankfully he was wrong. He was wrong about himself and about others. It would be the ultimate understanding for him. He is not who he fears he is. Faith tells me Hitler is built the same as me and every other human being. Our souls run on love. Hitler's soul was starved to death, but the solution is as simple as love. Everything about his life screamed out for love and acceptance. And though I believe it was always in front of him, his problem was in not seeing it; and that again is something I can understand, having suffered many times from similar fearful delusions.

But knowing all of this, am I not still telling a tale of failure due to fear? Faith says all things are good, right? How on earth can we see his atrocities as good? Well, let's looks at the alternatives. If we see this as a tragedy, then how must we see God? If we believe God failed Hitler and He failed the victims, how else could He fail us? Is He just as sick and demented as Hitler, since He created him? Or at least we have to recognize he ALLOWED those horrific things to happen.

The end result, IF you choose to see the Hitler situation as bad, is you end up with negativity and fear. Trust me I've thought through this every way possible. There's only one door leading out of the room of fear. And that's the doorway of faith.

Faith says everything that happened was for good. It was for everyone's good. It was one of the greatest learning experiences in the history of our world. If we can truly see what happened, we can actually find the secret to happiness itself! Through Hitler's example, we can see all the fears that tempt us to feel as he did. We can also see where it led him and how false it is.

I feel and believe right now, in another world, healing is happening for everyone involved. There is no other way out of it! God doesn't make mistakes! For him death is not the end we fear. Death is simply a change. Not something bad. Yes, you say, but look at HOW they died!

It's even easy to see the falsity behind this fear. People die in all different ways every day. To say that someone dying by gunshot, gas, or being brutally beaten is worse than someone getting into a car accident and being burned and mangled is pointless. What we're really trying to say is what makes it horrific is that it was intended by another human being. And while that's true, our only power is in understanding why. We can complain about the symptoms as much as we want, but until we begin to understand the cause, we are still stuck in the same situation with the same symptoms.

I believe the hearts of our generation are being opened for healing and understanding. The final proof I'll offer for this concept is simply this…try it in your heart. If you can muster the faith to let this new perspective sit in your heart, I KNOW you'll feel that absolute positive, creative, moving power of it. It's freeing and healing, and most of all, gives you power to move forward in happiness and strength.

With this faithful view, no longer am I a victim to the fear of Hitler. Most of all, I no longer have to fear the Hitler within me.

Now we're getting into the really good stuff! Here comes Disney!

CHAPTER 11

TM

WALT DISNEY – BUSINESS GENIUS OR THE ULTIMATE CULMINATION OF FAITH?

The inspiration to add Walt Disney to this book came in a unique way. I was nearly finished writing, when I received some advice from an editor that the Hitler section seemed a bit one-sided. It just so happens a few days previous, I'd done something out of the norm. I awoke as usual allowing my mind to be filled with all of my work responsibilities. But then I had the impression to try something new. I decided to ask my heart what I should do that day. I knew in that moment I was feeling like a victim to the tasks around me and knowing that victimization is a fear based result; I asked myself how I could feel differently. So with that in mind, I asked my heart what I should do that day. My heart said I should read the biography on Walt Disney I'd felt impressed to buy a few weeks previous.

So I did something I've never done before. I completely shirked all of my work responsibilities and sat down to a book. I read the entire day, and was blown away at how powerful Walt's story was. I was so completely uplifted by the energy I gleaned from this work, I couldn't wait to share it with my family and business partners. The wonderful book I'm speaking of is written by Bob Thomas and is entitled *Walt Disney: An American Original*.

When my editor mentioned the concern about the Hitler section, it hit me, I needed to contrast Hitler with Disney. It's literally like comparing night and day. As I researched Disney further, I was startled to find an amazing amount of similarity between these two men.

Disney, like Hitler, needs little introduction, though well-known for completely different reasons. For years, men have sought to decode and duplicate the success of this legend. Many good books have been written, but my look into the heart of this man will be unlike any other.

BOYHOOD

Walter Elias Disney was born to Flora and Elias Disney, Sunday, December 5, 1901, just 12 years after Adolph was born. Walt had three older brothers, Herb, Ray and Roy, and not long after he was born they had their first girl, Ruth. The family lived in Chicago at the time of Walt's birth but moved soon afterwards to Marceline, Missouri, where he spent his childhood years.

Walt was a curious, active, fun child who loved to explore the world around him. He had nothing but good memories of his life on their farm in Marceline. He spent his days helping his mother with chores and playing out on the farm.

In school, Walt's grades were only average. His teachers complained he was frequently distracted and had a hard time following the set curriculum. One time in art class they were required to draw a likeness of a bowl of flowers. When the teacher saw Walt's drawing she scolded him for not following directions. He had drawn faces on the flowers and arms instead of leaves.

Walt also came to love all forms of entertainment. At that time the main source of which was the Vaudeville shows and motion pictures. Walt loved any chance to sneak into a show, which he had to do without his father knowing. Afterwards he loved re-enacting the skits with friends.

Walt loved to draw and used his talent to get laughter from the locals with his cartoon strips.

A FATHER'S FEARS

Walt's father, Elias, was a good man who did his best to take care of his family, but like us all had his share of fear. As creative and fun-loving as Walt was, his father rarely was able to give him the attention to appreciate it. His mother balanced things out. She was kind, patient, loving and attentive, always there to laugh at his antics and support him.

Elias felt he had tried in every way to take care of his family. But his work life was stressful, going from one thing to another. Ironically like Adolph, Elias joined the military as a young married man, and when he felt like he needed to get back to his family, he walked out of the military camp and went home. Military police found him and went to arrest him for deserting, and like Adolph, Elias was able to talk his way out of it, stating there was no war so he was not deserting.

When he and Flora were first married, they owned an orange grove in Florida, a frost killed it and so Elias decided he would go in search of greener pastures. He went to Chicago and built houses and did fairly well, but the scare of crime in the big city drove him to Marceline to farm. In Marceline, they did well. However, Elias pushed his two oldest boys so hard they eventually became fed up and ran away. This was a major blow to Elias it seems he'd never recovered from. This event parallels Alois's experience with his first born son who also ran away from his father as a teen.

It was Roy's turn as a 16-year-old to become his father's right-hand man. Then, in the winter of 1909, Elias became ill with pneumonia and the burden of the farm fell entirely on Roy. It was too much for a young boy, and so again Elias moved, this time to Kansas City. Here he bought a paper route, and the majority of the burden would again fall on the two remaining boys Roy and Walt.

Elias was very firm and pushed them to perform no matter the conditions. Walt, being only 8-years-old, was required to arise at 3:30 each morning to deliver papers. This continued for six years, though rainstorms and blizzards. The boys were not allowed to ride bikes like some of the other paper boys. Elias feared losing business and insisted they go to each and every porch and lay the paper there neatly. Walt received a small allowance but was paid nothing for delivering the paper. *"Your pay is the room and board that I provide for you,"* Elias declared. Eventually Roy, like his older brothers, had enough. One summer night in 1912, he said goodbye to Walt with the words, *"Don't worry kid; everything will be all right here."*

Elias was further devastated by the rejection of his third son. And now that Walt was the only son left at home, he became the right hand-man for his father. When Elias decided to add a new kitchen and bedroom to their home, he insisted that Walt help him. Elias was quick to anger, so when Walt did something improperly he'd scold him, *"No, you don't saw the board that way, saw it like this!"*, and slap Walt on the rear end with the side of the saw.

One day Elias barked at Walt for not handing him a tool fast enough. Walt snapped back in defense. His father accused him of disrespect and ordered him to go to the basement for a thrashing. Roy, being home at the time, overheard the exchange and told Walt, *"Look, kid, he's got no reason for hitting you. You're fourteen years old. Don't take it anymore."* When Elias reached the basement, still in a rage, he grabbed a hammer handle and went to swing it at Walt. Walt grabbed it away from him. Elias raised his hand to strike him, and Walt held him by both wrists. Finally tears filled Elias's eyes and Walt loosened his grip and climbed the stairs. His father never tried to thrash him again.

Remember, anger and abuse isn't a black spot of evil within someone's heart. It's simply the lack or void of the positive. In the case of Elias, you can see the fear that filled his heart. I can see and relate to him as a father and how desperately he wanted to take care of and provide for his family. You can see how he could view himself as a failure in so many ways; this of course NOT being the truth, however. Fear is always a belief in a falsehood.

My father was a very kind and loving person, but like us all, he had a place of fear within him as a father. There was this certain line he'd drawn that was unspoken, but we knew it was there and we were not to cross it. We just knew if you crossed it, something bad would happen, that he'd "lose it", and so with fear he'd control us in this area. It was like there was one room in his heart that was locked and we were NOT allowed into it. It was this room of fear he guarded desperately.

Both my older brother Lance and I worked for my father. Being in our mid to late 20s at the time, we were beginning to experience some real friction in our relationship. It seemed to us as though we were expected to work twice as hard, twice as long, and for half as much as anyone else. That wasn't the reality, but it's how we felt.

The truth is we were struggling to find acceptance from our parents. We'd worked long and hard, and done much to improve the company, yet we never felt we could "get" what we needed from our parents. In fact, it felt as though the better we became and the more we accomplished, the less appreciation we'd receive, until it changed from lack of appreciation to criticism. No matter what we did, we were criticized and judged, which created the end result feeling of rejection.

We were confused and frustrated and spent most of our time arguing over things that were surface issues, never dealing with the real issues of fear. Finally one day, we recognized we couldn't have a relationship with my father based on fear and control any more. So we were sitting in Lance's office, he behind his desk and my father and I side by side on the other side. I remember us beginning to argue over the current state of affairs and my father's anger beginning to rise, which was our warning that we'd better back off. This time, however, instead of backing off, Lance pushed on. I watched in horror as my father became more and more angry. Then in response to the rising tide of anger, Lance simply stated, *"Dad, I'm not afraid of you."*

My father, now losing control, demanded, *"STOP IT!"* Again Lance responded calmly but firmly, *"I'm not afraid of you."* *"STOP IT!"* Dad warned louder. With calm resoluteness Lance responded again, *"I... am NOT afraid of you."* Finally my Dad came to his feet, face-to-face with my brother across the desk, his final warning. His face flushed red with anger unlike I'd ever seen. Lance, fearless of his tirade, looked him in his eyes, searching for the way past his anger and said, *"What are you going to do Dad, hit me?"*

I watched my father's angry determination turn to confusion and desperate searching. I could see the thoughts written across his face. He was thinking, *"He's right, what AM I going to do? Would I really hit my son? Why am I so angry anyway? Is it worth this awful situation?"* And then the realization came to him. *"It's over; I can no longer use fear and intimidation to control my sons."* It's as though Lance pulled back the curtain on the Wizard of Oz and found all that was behind the anger and intimidation was a sweet little man who just misunderstood his role as a leader.

My father's face began to drain, and he sat back into his chair, thoughtful. I began picking my jaw up off the floor. It was like watching the worst horror film and seeing the most amazing ending. And here was the best part of all. We didn't talk about it afterwards; we didn't need to. But what he learned that day was not only that he couldn't control us with fear, but even better, that he DIDN'T NEED TO! The very foundation of fear in our relationship said he didn't deserve our love or help, in and of himself. So he'd have to force it by other means. The truth was seen, he WAS deserving of our love, loyalty and service. We'd serve him to the very end! But the very thing that made us want to do it was being destroyed by his rejection of us, which was born of fear.

We were saying, "Dad we love you and want to work with you and for you, and the only thing that could ever ruin that for us is your rejection. Because all we want, all we need is your acceptance. We just want to hear you say, 'Son, you do a wonderful job, it's a privilege to work with you.'" He couldn't say that because he was too afraid if he said that, we'd get big heads and walk away from him. We'd go find a boss "worthy" of our talents and hard work.

Instead, in order to "keep" us, he'd downplay our accomplishments and talents and hold hostage that love and acceptance we fought so desperately for. It felt as though the carrot was always held just out of reach so that by this point we were starved and striving to communicate that if we didn't get some carrot, we're going somewhere where we could.

From this point on, our relationship was different. My father treated us more as partners and friends. Our relationship with him began to develop as he became able to accept we were there because we wanted to be, NOT because we were too scared to go somewhere else. Most of all, we worked with him because we loved him.

Reading into this situation between Walt and his father I can see Elias probably had mixed feelings about it. He was probably half grateful he no longer could use anger to control his son but half sad he'd been "called out" on his anger. I'm guessing that due to his fear, he chalked this up as another item on his long list of failures as a parent.

I find the similarity between Walt's and Adolph's fathers more than ironic. Were they really that different? Both were good men, trying to provide for their families. It was not some character flaw or spiritual defect that created the anger, it was simply fear. Fear that they weren't good enough, or their children wouldn't be good enough. They feared the inability to raise happy, successful children, though I know inside they were dying to be the loving parent their heart ached for. Fear, however, said it was a luxury they didn't get. Both fathers were obviously loved, but, since they viewed themselves as failures (to some extent) that love was nothing but a painful reminder how undeserving they were of it. Instead of placing their children in that same painful situation, they would teach their children the harsh reality of life, thereby protecting them from similar disappointment and pain.

Scarcity is another symptom of fear. Elias was an extraordinary spendthrift, he would walk miles rather than pay a nickel for the trolley. He rarely felt the freedom to spend money on anything other than absolute necessities. In fact, one rare instance where Elias actually took his wife and daughter to a local vaudeville show, there was a performer who balanced three chairs stacked over his head. The climax was a boy balancing on the top of the three chairs. They were startled to discover the boy was Walt. Because of his fears, Elias couldn't be supportive of Walt's interests, forcing Walt to sneak out his bedroom window in order to participate in various performances.

In his early teens Walt became more serious about understanding the world of entertainment, and began assembling a file of jokes he'd seen and thought up. He'd occasionally try out his best ones on his father, who'd listen without a smile. A couple days later, Elias would remark straight-faced to his son, *"You know, I've been thinking about that joke you told me, Walter. It's funny, very funny."* You see that big heart of his struggling to come out! You can see him struggling against his desire to be there and support his son, but the love of his heart is muffled by the walls of fear surrounding it.

As you can see both Adolph and Walt had fathers that couldn't be supportive of their son's natural talents and desires.

WALT FOLLOWS HIS HEART

As Walt's ambition to become a cartoonist began to flourish, Elias made it clear he didn't sympathize with it. However, he did agree to pay for some of Walt's art classes (just as Alois had for Adolph) if he agreed to get a job and help contribute to the family's income.

At the age of 15, Walt began his search for independence. Roy helped him get his first job selling convenience items to railroad passengers. This came to an abrupt end as Walt just couldn't seem to make a profit. While he took art classes, he found other jobs to help bring money into the family. He worked as a handyman and a night watchman in a jelly factory his father had invested in. Then he worked as a guard for the Wilson Avenue Elevated Railway. After finishing his freshman year of high school, he went to work for the post office. Finally, having a little extra money, Walt bought his first camera, which he used to photograph himself imitating one of his favorite characters, Charlie Chaplin.

Walt couldn't imagine attending another year of school; he was done with it. So at 16 years old Walt dropped out of school after the 9th grade (just as Adolph had). The First World War had started and Walt was anxious to serve his country. Two of his brothers had enlisted, and he was determined to as well. Walt's parents were not happy about his desire to enlist, to which he responded, *"I don't want my grandchildren asking me, Why weren't you in the war? Were you a slacker?"* Though Walt was too young to enlist, he found if he forged the year of his birth by one year, he could get into the Red Cross.

This became another bitter subject between Walt and his father, who vehemently refused to sign the papers allowing him to participate. He claimed signing it would be signing a death warrant for his son. Flora argued, that due to his stubbornness they'd already lost three of their sons without warning. She'd rather sign it and know where he was then lose contact with another son. Elias still refused, so she forged his name.

Walt was shipped to Paris, France, where he served in the Red Cross. This is the same war Adolph was so extremely excited to participate in from the other side. Walt served as a driver at the canteen, with the job to run errands. There was a group of German prisoners, who worked there as well.

Ironically, Walt became friends with the German prisoners who'd play jokes on him. One time, they tricked Walt into buying wine they claimed was for one of Walt's superiors. He later found them having a great time with the wine he'd purchased.

One prisoner Walt grew close to was named Rupert. When the prisoners went on work crews, Walt and Rupert would sit in the canteen car and talk about the war and the future of Germany. One day, they drove to the outskirts of the village, where the German prisoners were to load wood onto trucks. French children walked by on their way home from school and started throwing rocks at the prisoners. Walt told Rupert, who spoke French, to order the children to stop. They persisted however, so Walt told the prisoners to fill their pockets with rocks. When the children ignored the second command to stop, Walt called out *"Rupert, charge!"* The prisoners loosed a barrage of rocks and chased the children into the village.

What was it that gave Walt the power to see the Germans as people instead of enemies? Were they not at war? Did Walt not realize the deaths of his own people? Why didn't he so naturally see things as black or white, good or bad, as so many others did? The answer is deep within his heart. It had everything to do with how he saw himself. It had everything to do with the Ancient Greek aphorism, "Know Thyself". I'm sure you've heard of this statement, but what does it mean? This statement rests on the foundational belief we are all alike, created from the same source, having the same heart. And so if you "know yourself" you actually come to know all mankind as well.

It's pretty simple from here. Picture an individual who views himself negatively. What must he assume of everyone else? Essentially, if he fears himself, he must fear everyone else. And because he feels insecure within himself, he cannot give anything but insecurity to others.

Walt, on the other hand, had this uncommon faith within himself. Not an organized religious faith. In fact, he claimed a heavy dose of religion as a child discouraged him from it, and he especially didn't like sanctimonious preachers (preachers who pretended to be religious, virtuous or righteous, or in other words, were a fake). It's uncanny how Walt could sense insecurity being a form of fear, and be so averse to it. This is why Walt never put anything of organized religion into his films. At the same time, Walt didn't put religion down; he actually admired some aspects of it and supported his daughters as they went to different churches, leaving the choice completely up to them.

Walt's faith, however, was a different kind. It was the faith in himself and who he was. It was as if he didn't get why everyone else struggled with fear. With this foundation it all becomes simple. "I see myself as good, and so everyone else must be as well." There, of course, were times when Walt was frustrated with other individuals, but as a foundation, this is where Walt stood.

Back to Walt in the war, during his downtime in the Red Cross, Walt would draw cartoons and submit them to the leading humor magazines at the time. All were politely rejected. When he was at the age of 18, the war ended and Walt returned home to start his career, this time to Chicago where his parents had recently moved.

STEPPING OUT IN FAITH

Walt was finally home, nearly an adult, with his life ahead of him. Elias wanted to "help" his returned son find a good stable job. And just like Alois, Elias's fear said, "Walt can't make it on his own, I have to help him with what I've accomplished, or else he'll fail and suffer as I have." So he offered his son a job at the local jelly factory he was a part of and in which he'd invested his life savings. Walt replied, *"Dad, I don't want that kind of job."* Elias reminded him thousands of unemployed veterans would welcome such a position. Walt remained firm.

Notice the scare tactic used by referring to ALL of the UNEMPLOYED veterans. He's hinting that if he doesn't take this job, he may never find another. Remember Alois did the very same thing, pressuring Adolph to get into the civil servant profession as he had where he could help him. Again, this isn't something bad, it's simply the combination of good intentions mixed with fear.

Finally Elias said, *"Then what do you want to do, Walter?"* *"I want to be an artist."* Walt replied. *"And how do you expect to make a living as an artist?"* Elias questioned. *"I don't know,"* Walt simply admitted, and against his father's wishes, left for Kansas City to pursue his dream.

Notice how surprisingly similar Walt and Adolph's lives are to this point. Both wanted to be artists. Both struggled with fearful fathers though balanced by loving mothers. Both lived during the same period of time under very similar financial circumstances. So far, if we want to make a case that we are solely the product of our upbringing, we'd have a huge hole right in the middle of it.

After several rejections, Walt found his first job with *Pesmen-Rubin Commercial Art Studio.* They were so impressed with Walt's energy and work they hired him on the spot. Here Walt drew art for signs and advertisements. Another young man named Ub Iwerks came to work with Walt and they became good friends. However, as demand decreased, both boys were let go and had to seek other employment. They decided to go into business together; Walt drained his savings of $500 to start it and they called their enterprise *"Iwerks-Disney."* The venture only lasted a month when Walt found another full time job as cartoonist. Ub came to work for the same firm, named *Film-Ad,* not long afterward.

Film-Ad was what Walt had been looking for. They made cartoons for motion pictures and he immediately immersed himself into the job. Soon he was coming up with ways to improve the process and make the images more life-like and smooth in motion. His employers were thrilled with his work, and Walt began to improve nearly every part of the process with his enthusiasm. He even began injecting his own humor into the scripts he felt were lacking.

Walt's mind was going full speed and he couldn't learn enough in the field he loved. So he asked his manager if he could borrow one of the company's stop-action cameras to do some experimenting on the side. The manager refused, but Walt insisted until he gave in. Walt enlisted his older brother Roy to help him set up a make-shift studio in a garage. Walt created his own short animated film and took it to a local theater owner. The owner liked it and commissioned Walt to make him a new one every week. Walt was ecstatic, until he realized the price he told the theater owner was just his cost to make the films. It left him no profit.

But this didn't change Walt's view of himself. *Oh well,* he thought and kept going. Walt continued to make his cartoons on the side and started to gain attention as people began to notice his talented efforts.

Around this time, Elias met "failure" again. The jelly factory he'd invested his life savings into went bankrupt and the company president was imprisoned for fraud. Again, Elias sought to improve his fortune by moving on; this time back to Kansas City.

This is further evidence of Elias's fear of failure. For one, starting over in a place where you already have relationships should be much easier than starting from scratch. But because he saw these events as failures, he couldn't bear to live near the people he feared would see him as such. He had to get away to clean the slate and hide his failure.

The truth is, there is no failure, there is only learning and growth; a belief we see in Walt's eyes. This is why the fear of failure is an illusion. It's easy to see when you look at doing anything new in life. In order to learn how to do something new, you make what we call "mistakes", but "mistakes" are not little failures, they are just steps leading to the end result. Had Edison seen all of his steps leading to the invention of the light bulb as failures, he'd have stopped. In fact he'd have proved himself one of the biggest failures in history because it happened hundreds, if not thousands of times! No, he saw the truth, there is no such thing as failure, only learning, growth and progression.

Walt eventually outgrew the garage and rented a small shop. He advertised for boys who wanted to learn the cartoon business. He found three whom he taught in the evenings. He told the boys he couldn't afford to pay them but promised them a part of future profits he was sure would be there.

His films were called *Laugh-O-grams*, and Walt started making longer cartoons based on fairy tales, modernized with humor. The first was *Little Red Riding Hood*, which Walt was so pleased with he quit his job at *Film-Ad*. Walt collected $15,000 from local investors and hired five more young animators and a few other employees. He also talked Ub into coming to work with him. They rented a small five-room suite in an office building and went to work.

They eventually made a deal with a distribution company out of New York for $11,000 for six cartoons. After many months, and the completion of the six cartoons, the news came that their New York Distributor had gone bankrupt and the only money they received was the $100 deposit they were paid to start. As salaries dwindled, Walt lost his employees and was left on the verge of bankruptcy. He couldn't afford rent, so he lived in the *Laugh-O-grams* offices.

There was no bath, so once a week he made the journey to the railway station where he paid ten cents for a warm bath and bar of soap. After the bath, he'd stand on the platform where he'd seen his parents, sister and Roy depart for the west. He wept, later stating, *"It was so lonesome."* He ate on credit at the Greek owned café downstairs from his office. At one point he couldn't keep up with his tab and one of the café partners told him he could no longer eat there. Two days later, the other partner found Walt sitting on a box, eating beans from a can and said, *"Oh, Walter I don't care what my partner says. You go downstairs and get something to eat."*

Walt was given the opportunity to create a short cartoon for a local dentist. When the dentist asked him to come to his house to complete the deal, Walt had to admit his only pair of shoes was being repaired and he didn't have the $1.50 to get them back. The dentist paid the bill and Walt created *Tommy Tucker's Tooth* for $500.

Walt signed another deal with a distribution company to film a unique cartoon that included a live girl. It was titled *Alice's Wonderland*. Unfortunately, halfway through the production, Walt was broke and he had to write a letter to the distribution company stating he wouldn't be able to complete the cartoon.

Walt described his situation to Roy who was at this point in a hospital with tuberculosis; where he would spend five years, recovering. Roy responded to Walt's letter, *"Kid, I think you should get out of there. I don't think you can do any more for it."* Walt resigned himself to bankruptcy. Another cartoon maker offered

Walt a job, but Walt wanted to leave the scene of his failure.

Does this sound familiar? Walt was taught when something like this happens it's called failure and you can't show your face in that society any more. Roy knew it as well, since he even recommends to Walt, *get out of there*.

Walt, seeing this as failure, decided he would leave cartooning behind him and become a director in Hollywood. He raised money by going door to door taking pictures of babies and then he sold his camera to buy a ticket to California. He had $40 cash, his imitation-leather suitcase with only one shirt, two undershorts, two pair of socks and some drawing materials. However, the ticket he bought was first-class!

Notice how unknowingly Walt assumed some of his father's fears. Yet in this very instance, we see small acts of rejection of this fear. Here Walt buys a first-class ticket...why? Despite what may have appeared to be happening to Walt from the outside, something else was brewing on the inside. Deep down, Walt didn't believe he was a failure. Walt's faith burned like a warm stove ignorant of the cold winter storm outside. Walt knew who he was. He saw his worth separate from money, from status, and from what others might think or say. He made a conscious decision to re-validate his worth by purchasing that first-class ticket, because in his mind, that's just what he was...first-class.

MOVING TO HOLLYWOOD

It was now 1923, and Walt was 22 when he arrived in Hollywood. Walt moved in with his retired uncle, Robert, in Los Angeles, and immediately began searching the town for a position as director. Everyone seemed unimpressed by the young inexperienced man. He was turned down every time. It was unlike Walt to lose faith but he continued to see his previous experience as a failure and struggled to start over with something that maybe he would be good at.

The failure philosophy says if you don't "succeed" at something then you've "failed". It's a black-and-white mentality that prevents us from progression. Because Walt saw this as failure, he sat at a crossroad. If he continued in this belief, he would no longer follow his heart and his passion. Once you stray off that path, the confused beliefs you hold to be true dam you. Walt's heart had already told him what he was supposed to do. Just like his father found passion and success in many things he'd done in his life. But each time the beast of failure reared its scary head, Elias had to lower his, admit defeat and try something else. For example, had he continued in the construction business he'd found immediate success with in Chicago, he may have not known financial insecurity

Walt went to visit Roy in the nearby hospital in West Los Angeles and told him of his frustration. Roy suggested Walt return to the cartoon business. Can we all say a big thank you to Roy? Don't you just love him? Up to this point, Roy has believed and supported Walt all the way. It began as children, when Roy pushed baby Walter in a buggy carriage up and down their Chicago neighborhood, unashamed. When Walt and Elias came into conflict, it was Roy who believed in Walt enough to tell him to stand up. Numerous times Roy gave Walt money...to start his first job, to help him when Laugh-o-grams was failing, and for the rest of their career it would be Roy's destiny to continue supporting his brother, emotionally and financially. A key factor to success is to surround yourself with faithful people. People who see as much or more than you see in yourself.

To Roy's suggestion, Walt complained, *"No, I'm too late. I should have started six years ago. I don't see how I can top those New York boys now."* Walt left, feeling discouraged, sitting at this critical junction of his life, unemployed, and living off his uncle.

Mentally at this point, Walt is feeding both of the wolves of faith and fear, but we see him feed the faith a little more as he concludes the only way of breaking into the movie business is with cartoons! He began by rigging up a cartoon stand in his Uncle Robert's garage, using dry-goods boxes and spare lumber. Then he set out to find a patron.

He visited the office of Alexander Pantages, who owned a chain of theaters, and outlined his idea to Alexander's assistant. *"Mr. Pantages wouldn't be interested,"* the assistant claimed. *"How do you know I wouldn't be interested?",* came a voice from behind. It was Mr. Pantages. He became Walt's first customer.

Notice how difficult the path became as Walt strayed from it. It was like he was lost in a vast road-less wasteland, looking for meaning; but the moment he stepped back onto his path of faith, instantly he begins seeing the signs and confirmations he's on the right track. This was ONLY possible because he turned away from his fear of failure and got back on his horse.

Next, Walt decides to try to finish the *Alice's Adventure Series* for his cartoon distributor, Margaret Winkler in New York. He contacts Miss Winkler about the possibility. Walt received the reply late one night and rushed to the hospital to tell his brother. Roy awoke to Walt standing over him smiling and waving a piece of paper. *"What's the matter?"* Roy whispered. *"We're in! It's a deal!"* Walt exclaimed. Walt proposed Roy leave the hospital and partner with him. After thinking it over, Roy left the hospital the next morning never to return.

Roy assumed the financial roll immediately by applying to banks for loans, but they all refused claiming cartoons were too risky. Roy finally turned to Uncle Robert who objected pointing to Walt's previous "failure". Roy's faith and persistence prevailed, however, and Uncle Robert loaned $500 for his nephew's enterprise.

THE DISNEY BROTHERS, IN BUSINESS

Walt and Roy began the exciting process of building their new business, Walt Disney Studios. They outgrew one building after another. Walt contacted his old friends back in Kansas City, and talked most of them into moving to sunny California, Ub being one of them.

Here we see the true Walt come out. The way he developed his business was unlike what we'd normally expect. We think of business as a simple mathematical calculation, you spend less than you make and that becomes rule number one. Because face it, if you spend more than you make, you'll be out of business, right?

We get another glimpse into Walt's heart. This was not rule number one to him. Rule number one to him was making the best damn cartoon possible! This meant every penny that came in he'd spend on making the highest quality product they possibly could. And it meant every time they increased their income, they would increase their spending on their product. From one perspective, you could really say it wasn't about the money. How amazing is that? But the big question is HOW? How was he like that?

As abnormal as this may seem, it really is more common than we may realize. You see, all men are like Walt at their core. We all want to do something great. The one thing that stops us before we even begin is, of course, our fear. Walt knew who he was, and so he had little fear of himself. That means he overcame his fear of failure. Instead, he worked in the faith that if he gave it all he had, he would create something wonderful. He didn't fear money, because he didn't fear failure. And he worked on a higher plane. He worked on the plane of faith which said, "If I put everything I have into creating the absolute best for myself and for others, the money will be there." It's the act of faith that steps out into the seeming nothingness and is rewarded with solid ground.

Walt began forming a process and culture that would never change. He would use processes that were the "best". That meant if there was a way they could speed up the creation process but it hurt the quality in any way, then they would NOT do it. This didn't mean he did things the expensive way just to spend money. No, he was adamant that they unceasingly pushed the envelope to find better, faster and less expensive ways to create his visions. When new technologies became available, he was the first to adopt. And when the technology wasn't there, he'd find a way to create it himself. And from this point forward, that vision never changed.

Also, he never gave the responsibility of vision away. This was the key to the forming of this legendary company. Because the absolute secret ingredient to his success was one thing...his heart and his faith, which created his vision; he knew this could never be given away because it was only his.

This didn't stop him from spreading his vision to everyone he came in contact with. It was more than just unusual he could talk almost anyone into working with him. They didn't even know why, except that when he spoke, you just knew he was right. He easily talked his former artists into moving to the other side of the continent and changing their entire life for him. It is so evident that when he spoke, people believed him, but why?

Walt had faith in himself. This is a truth and your heart will recognize truth whenever it hears it. This faith was completely infectious because it was truth. When he spoke, people listened, because he had what everyone is looking for. He had faith in himself. And everyone is drawn to it. It's a powerful energy, because when one person is that secure, the energy they give off is security. Everyone wants to be secure. It's just that most of us don't know how. Walt had it, and this was the "Midas Touch" that began the creation of an empire.

During this period of time, Walt began courting Lillian Bounds, a pretty girl who worked as a painter in his studio. Roy took Walt to a cut-rate jeweler who displayed a $75 three-quarter-carat diamond surrounded by tiny blue sapphires, as well as other rings at $35. July 13, 1925 Walt placed the $75 ring on Lily's finger and they were married.

Despite Walt's faith, fear still existed in the individuals around him. And after a couple years, *The Alice Series* had run its course. Walt's contact, Margaret Winkler, had married a man named Charlie Mintz. Mintz took over the business, and became a major source of negativity to the Disney business. When Walt would submit his latest film Mintz's response was usually very critical. Rarely did he give positive feedback; most of the time he was pressuring Walt either to make better cartoons or reduce the price.

Walt came up with a new series, *Oswald the Rabbit*. Initially what came from Mintz was more criticism, but eventually it was more than evident the series was doing well. Walt approached Mintz for a much-deserved price increase. Walt had continued to invest more and more into the business, increasing his cost to make the films, without any increase in price.

When Walt proposed a price increase, Mintz told him not only would he not increase the price, but he'd cut the price by almost a third. Walt was stunned. Mintz then pulled out his hidden ace; recently he'd contacted each of Walt's artists, except Ub, and had them sign an agreement to work for him. He convinced them he owned the rights to Oswald, so if they wanted a job, they'd have to work for him. Mintz took Walt's staff and the cartoon he'd created.

At this point, Walt is in New York in negotiations with Mintz while trying to communicate with an anxious Roy, who was concerned about what was happening. We get to see inside Walt's mind through his communication with Roy. He let Roy know initially, *"Mintz is determined to get absolute control of everything, and will do everything in his power to gain his end. But unknown to him, we have a stronger power on our side."*

I can't help but smile as I feel faith permeate his words. Here he has this large distribution company totally manipulating and quite frankly, working to destroy him, and he says *"we have a stronger power on our side."* What was the power he's talking about? Was it God? Well, not in an organized religious sense. But it definitely was faith. A simple belief...and he was absolutely right. He DID have a stronger power!

Later he says to Roy, *"...don't worry. I really do FEEL that everything will turn out all right."* What classic words! Notice first of all what this does for Roy. It takes away his fear...with the simple words, *don't worry*. Walt's got it going on, he knows what fear will do to them. Then he says, *"I REALLY DO FEEL that everything will turn out all right."* This is a simple yet POWERFUL statement of truth and faith. He emphasizes his faith with the word *really*. And then he uses the word *feel*.

This is a key word because *feel* is the word we use to reference our heart; a sincere belief that is core to us. Our heart is the testing station of our soul for truth. When we *feel* something is right, it means it has passed the truth test. Again here we plainly see Walt isn't using some shrewd business technique to manipulate the situation in his direction. He doesn't have some carefully laid out plan for just this type of situation where he can pull out his own ace to turn the tables on Mintz. No he's simply following his heart.

Then his last line to Roy is, *"Anyways I believe that whatever does happen is FOR THE BEST."* Again all you can say is...what a stud. And this is not just Walt having a positive attitude; it's so much more than that. It's Walt seeing the truth of himself in every situation. If you see yourself as a securely successful person, you don't fear failure. Walt didn't fear failure; he only sought to create the success he already knew he was. Again faith sees ALL things as good. This was his secret power.

Finally, Walt approached Mintz and gave him the rights to Oswald. It's recorded Walt showed no bitterness or anger toward Mintz. In fact, he left him with the words, *"Protect yourself, Charlie. If my artists did it to me, they'll do it to you."*

If you suspect Walt showed ignorance in any way, here you see how open his eyes truly are. Walt understood the principle of fear very well. People are easily manipulated through fear, and since Mintz had done this to them, he'd created a cycle of negativity. He'd used the power of fear to get what he wanted, or in other words what he thought was a positive result. However, Walt knew you can never use negative energy and get positive results. And he was right, that negative energy came back to Mintz and he did end up losing the artists he had stolen.

Even more important let's look at how Walt dealt with the situation inwardly. He didn't lash out at Mintz; he didn't fight back with him. Theoretically, Walt could have spent the rest of his career fighting with Mintz over the rights to what he'd created. No, Walt worked in a different world. A world where he knew he had to stay in a state of positive energy. Walt didn't fear Mintz to be an evil person he needed to bring to justice.

Again we see Walt's faithful view of mankind. It's evidenced by his final words to Mintz, he only felt sorry Mintz worked in a state of fear, because that type of dishonestly and betrayal can only be driven by fear. Mintz feared he wouldn't make enough money, or that Walt was so good he'd have to pay more money or that Walt's films were so good he'd lose them to another distributor. So he worked out what he thought in his fearful mind was a clever and shrewd business move. And because he feared losing Oswald, that's eventually what happened.

A Merry Mouse is Born

Walt saw the situation for what it was, and walked away. He didn't allow it to form fear in his heart of other men, he simply saw Mintz as scared. He knew himself, and walked away to more success because that's who he was…successful. His final telegram to Roy said *"…don't worry everything ok will give details when arrive – Walt."*

When Walt arrived at the train station, he gave no hint of the situation that could have been viewed by Roy as tragic. It wasn't until Roy finally asked, *"Tell me about it, kid-- what kind of deal did you make?"*

"We haven't got a deal", Walt admitted cheerfully. But before Roy could

begin to fear, Walt quickly added: *"We're going to start a new series."* Walt then related to Roy that on the train ride home he'd already been inspired with a character for a new series. Walt was inspired by a mouse that ran around his drawing table back in his Kansas City office. He wanted to name it Mortimer Mouse but Lily didn't like the name and suggested Mickey instead. Thus the merry mouse was born!

How interesting to recognize Walt was inspired with the vision of Mickey Mouse on the train ride home from Mintz in New York. Walt had to let go of Oswald, to make room for Mickey. The act of "letting go" was a demonstration of faith all would be okay. Thus, Mickey was brought to Walt's mind. The act of letting go of something that isn't going to work only makes room for the next inspiration. Letting go is a key to success, and faith is the power to do so.

Because the Disney Studio was still producing the last film for the *Oswald* series with the artists that had agreed to go to work for Mintz, Walt had to begin production on the first Mickey Mouse cartoon, titled *Plane Crazy,* with Ub in secrecy. Once the *Oswald* series was finished, Walt, Roy, and Ub had the studio to themselves and their new mouse. The first Mickey Mouse cartoon was finished, and Walt instructed Ub to start the next one, *The Gallopin' Gaucho.* Walt still had not found a distributor for the Mickey Mouse cartoons but was already interested in a brand new concept.

"SOUND" FAITH

Up to this point, all motion pictures were silent, with only captions for messages. Walt had heard about some companies putting sound in sync with the picture. Ironically other cartoon producers at the time actually feared that adding sound would somehow ruin the illusion of their cartoon on the screen when the characters opened their mouths to speak. A sign of fear in your life is lack of motion. Fear is damning. Because these producers feared change, Walt sprung ahead of them.

Walt concluded, *"Sound effects and talking pictures are more than a mere novelty. They are here to stay and in time will develop into a wonderful thing."* And so even though the first two cartoons hadn't found a buyer yet, Walt planned a third that would be synchronized with sound, *Steamboat Willie.*

Again here we have another decision made that sent him ahead of others. What gave him the fuel for that decision? Was it genius? Was it shrewdness? No, in fact it wasn't even necessarily that he was moving past the others. It was that the others were stopped by their fear and Walt wasn't.

So Walt made a journey to New York to find the equipment he'd need to add sound to his third Mickey Mouse cartoon. When it came to sound the production industry was a mess. And Walt had trouble finding the equipment he needed. Some recommended solutions Walt knew weren't long term, and so he continued to search for what he felt was the right way to do it. Eventually he found a distributor that had a product which met his specifications. He then set to work finding an orchestra. Being one of the first to ever perform this feat, Walt had to figure out his own system of synchronization. He created a time system of twenty-four frames of film per second synched with music, sound effects and the minimal dialogue he himself performed.

By this point, Walt had been away from his wife for weeks and was feeling homesick and worn out by the whole situation. He shows signs of over-exposure to negative energy as he writes home, *"This damn town is enough to give anybody the heebie jeebies. I sure wish I was home."* Despite this feeling, Walt counteracts it with a faithful request to have Ub go forward with the fourth Mickey Mouse cartoon, *The Barn Dance*.

Walt finally found a director and orchestra, but had more setbacks as the director of the orchestra wanted to record it his way but couldn't get the timing right. This recording session wasn't successful, and they didn't have the money to do it again. Roy worked to raise more but was unsuccessful. At this point Walt could have seen failure coming again like a freight train, but instead he writes Roy and Ub this message, *"I am figuring on a good release. I don't think we will have any trouble getting it; this may mean the making of a big organization out of our little dump. Why should we let a few dollars jeopardize our chances? I think this is Old Man Opportunity rapping at our door. Let's don't let the jingle of a few pennies drown out his knock. See my point? So slap as big a mortgage on everything we got and let's go after this thing in the right manner."* With that, Walt also gave permission to sell his beloved Moon Roadster.

In another message he wrote later, he proclaims, *"Are we downhearted? HELL NO."* The hell no was typed in red.

It's so important to see what's really going on here. Walt is facing what most people would consider to be their greatest fears; financial ruin, failure, the letting down of his family, friends and co-workers and most of all, himself.

Yet he's leading by faith, no matter how bleak the situation appears. He doesn't let fear become a decision maker in his life. He also intuitively understood the prophetic words of another icon of success, Bruce Lee, who said: *"Don't fear failure. — Not failure, but low aim, is the crime. In great attempts it is glorious even to fail."* Now I don't think it's because he really doesn't ever feel afraid. No, I absolutely believe he was pretty dang nervous at this point. But when it came down to the decision, he made it in faith, not out of fear.

Walt was also a master, whether he knew it or not, at managing not only his own fear but the fear of his partners. He instinctively knew the power of faith and carefully worked to manufacture and distribute this priceless energy to the people who help him build his dream.

Eventually, Walt's faith was fulfilled as he filmed a bouncing ball on the screen to give the director the correct rhythm, and the piece was finally recorded successfully! Walt's *Steamboat Willie* had sound! Now all he had to do was find a buyer.

Walt went to all the major film distribution companies. They all politely declined the film. Again, it was another point fear could have easily told Walt, "This is the end. You've contacted all the distributors and they don't want it; you're finished, bankrupt, a failure…again." But faith doesn't see the obstacles, it sees the way around the obstacles.

This is another perfect example of a principle taught by Bruce Lee. Here's what Lee called the Principle of the Power of Fluid; *Be like water making its way through cracks. Do not be assertive, but adjust to the object, and you shall find a way round or through it. If nothing within you stays rigid, outward things will disclose themselves. Empty your mind; be formless, shapeless, like water. If you put water into a cup, it becomes the cup. You put water into a bottle and it becomes the bottle. You put it in a teapot it becomes the teapot. Now, water can flow or it can crash. Be water my friend.*

Water doesn't see obstacles, it only sees the way around them. In this case Walt, as Bruce Lee advises, becomes like water and looks for the way around the obstacle; and sure enough he finds it. He runs into a theater owner who explains, speaking of the distribution companies, *"Those guys don't know what's good until the public tells them."* He suggested Walt get *Steamboat Willie* into his theater and *"let the audience sell it for you"*. Believe it or not, Walt's initial reply was, *"Gee, I don't know. I'm* **afraid** *that if I run it at a Broadway house, it'll take the edge off my chances to sell it to a distributor."*

It's re-assuring to know even Walt wasn't always perfectly faithful. However, he allowed faith to make the final decision, and he agreed to let it show. November 18, 1928, *Steamboat Willie* opened at the *Colony Theater*, and it was the sensation Walt dreamed it would be. The local papers heralded it as a hit, and at last the distribution companies were calling Walt to come in and discuss a deal. However, this time Walt would not give up the rights to Mickey Mouse as he had with *Oswald*. He held out until he got the deal he felt was right. The deal he made for the distribution of the *Mickey Mouse* cartoons was with a man named Pat Powers who would prove to be another test of Walt's faith.

Walt's faith was again rewarded as *Mickey Mouse* soon became a national hit. *Mickey Mouse* clubs were popping up all over the country in 1929. In fact it became a catch phrase for theaters not playing a Disney cartoon, *"What – no Mickey Mouse?"*

MOVING FORWARD IN FAITH

Walt's vision continues to grow. He came up with a new series called the *Silly Symphonies*. This series allowed him more latitude in creativity. But as he finished his first *Silly Symphony*, he again got to deal with the realty of being a visionary among the visionless. Pat Powers, his distributor, turned down the film with the words, *"They don't want this. More mice."*

Walt again went around the obstacle by showing *The Skeleton Dance*, his first *Silly Symphony* in a downtown Los Angeles theater. The crowd responded well but the owner said it was too gruesome. Walt showed it to two other theaters where the response was as he suspected...overwhelming, and Pat Powers again was convinced.

Just a year later, Walt and Roy found Pat wasn't sending them royalties for the films. Walt met with Powers, who blew off his demands for an audit of receipts and then dropped the bombshell he'd stolen Ub Iwerks by offering increased pay. He then demanded that if Walt wanted to keep Ub he'd have to sign an agreement giving Powers control. Pat Powers, like Mintz, sought out of fear to use fear to control Disney.

"Look," Powers said, *"you and your brother need money. I'll make you a deal that will relieve you of the concern about money matters. I'll pay you a weekly salary. I'm willing to go as high as twenty-five hundred dollars a week."* This was Powers attempt to take control of what he knew was a golden goose. However, Powers was shocked at Walt's response, assuming Walt was like most other men, easily controlled by fear. Walt didn't think twice about Pat's offer. He was only concerned about his long time friend Ub who did got to work with Powers.

As a side note Walt and Roy had made Ub a 20% partner in *Walt Disney Studios*. He sold his portion for $2,920 when he left. Had he stayed, hypothetically speaking, his market value would have reached $7,000,000,000!

The Disney brothers were impacted by another negatively focused individual. How they reacted is everything. They again were faced with the same choice. Do we leave or fight? They chose to walk away, despite the fact Powers owed them tens of thousands. The Disney's also agreed to pay Pat Powers

$100,000 for the release of the twenty-one cartoons he was in possession of. Walt's faith led him through this difficult decision, knowing that to stay and fight would be a waste of time and energy he could be putting to positive use. He showed us over and over he would make a conscious choice to remain in a state of positive energy. He dodged the negative that was thrown at him instead of getting wrapped up in it. It's also important to note that a key product of faith is movement. Think of the implication of the words, "He walked away." It's movement.

It's perfectly fitting Walt chose to reproduce Joseph Campbell's classic tale of *Brer Rabbit and the Tar Baby*. If you don't recall, the story begins with Brer Fox, who dislikes Brer Rabbit, but no matter what he tries, he just can't seem to catch him. So Brer Fox devises a scheme to trap the bunny. He creates a tar baby. When Brer Rabbit approaches and says, "Howdy", the baby offends him by not replying. Here, a fear of Brer Rabbit's becomes exposed. He's offended the baby doesn't respond. Notice how fear is always founded in illusion and falsehood. The tar baby isn't even real. It can't respond. So the problem exists solely within the Rabbit.

As his fear of being disrespected becomes evident, the Rabbit threatens to punch the tar baby; which he does. And sure enough his hand gets stuck. Blinded by his fear and viewing the fact the tar baby won't let go as further proof of his fear, he swings his other fist…stuck. Then he kicks…stuck. Finally he head-butts the tar baby, completely paralyzing himself. Brer Fox walks up as pleased as peaches. Laying a fear trap worked like a charm.

Walt knew no matter whether you were right or wrong, wasting time in negative energy does nothing by paralyze your ability to perform positively. This certainly wasn't an excuse for weakness, or the inability to fight. It is, in fact, the greatest form of strength and wisdom.

Not only did Walt walk away from negativity that would have robbed us of the fruits of his positive energy, but he was rewarded again with something even better. It was always Walt's faith, his belief that whatever happens was for the best. And that belief came to fruition every time. This time, it was in landing a new distribution deal with Columbia. It was by far the best deal they'd had so far, and most of all, it allowed them to keep moving forward! And that's just what they did.

PEACE, FAITH'S FRUIT

It's at this point in 1931 we see Walt's faith tested. Walt begins to overwhelm himself and the people he worked with. His entire working career was him pushing as fast and as hard as he could go. He'd regularly work from early morning till late into the night. He began to grow impatient with anything less than perfection, and would even snap at co-workers. Sudden disappointment could easily plunge him into a fit of tears. This led to an emotional break-down. His doctor gave him the sound advice that he needed to get away from work for a period of time, which he did. And after a long vacation with his sweetheart, the first in five years, he returned completely rested and rejuvenated.

So what were Walt's fears that were breaking him down emotionally? It's a fear I'm coming to understand well. When use the faith to live your dreams you face one of the greatest fears of all. You see failing at something you don't believe is what you were truly meant to do is not a big deal. Especially compared to living and creating what you feel with all your soul you were meant to. Here is where you face real fears. Fears that most don't know exists. Our natural tendancy is to hold that deep inspired idea way out of light so that we can always fall back on it. It's like the singer who never let their light shine. Deep inside they can always comfort themselves with the thought, "I could have been a world famous vocalist." But to actually test that belief would mean risking failure.

When you really choose to live your dreams you will be forced to face the fear of failure. The fear says you can't accomplish these grand wonderful dreams in your head and life is going to pass you by. You'll miss your chance. It becomes a fear of time, resources and energy. It can cause you to fall into a scarcity mindset. So what was the cure?

Walt made a conscious decision to refute this fear by replying to it with the fact that there IS enough time, resources and energy. I'll prove my belief in this by taking a significant chunk of time off. It allowed him to let go. It also helped to curb this fear by him remembering his true worth. There's not a better way to do this than to be with the one you love. They took the time to recognize and celebrate the wonderful life they ALREADY HAD! It wasn't something he had to keep pushing for, because it was already there. He reminded himself he wasn't working to be happy. Instead he was happy first, and this gave him the desire and strength to work at creating something wonderful.

After this experience, Walt learned the importance of fostering this type of faith. From then on, he took time to exercise, play golf, polo and leave work earlier to spend more time with his wife and family. Finding this day-to-day peace became an essential part of his life.

The Dream Grows

Walt's amazing faith continued to bear fruit and by 1931, *Mickey Mouse* was known in every civilized country. In London, Madame Tussaud's museum enshrined Mickey in wax. Mrs. Franklin D. Roosevelt wrote to Walt from the White House: *"My husband is one of the devotees of Mickey Mouse… Please believe that we are all most grateful to your for many delightful evenings."* The Disneys were even awarded a medal from the League of Nations for *Mickey Mouse*. Notice how the simple faith of one man touched an entire world.

In 1934, Walt had seen vast success with his cartoon shorts, but he had a new dream. He decided it was time to create the first-ever, animated, full-length, feature film. Walt's artists first found out about the new project one night after dinner. They returned to work and found Walt waiting for them in the auditorium. He asked them to sit down in chairs set in a semi-circle around him and he commenced to tell the story of *Snow White*.

The way he told a story is legendary. He'd immerse himself into each role, playing the part meticulously. His eyes twisted in an evil way depicting the wicked witch, his face would beam as he played the dwarfs. The performance took two hours, and at the end when the Prince's kiss awakened the sleeping Snow White, there were tears in the eyes of his listeners. *"That is going to be our first feature,"* Walt announced.

Immediately, Walt met the usual fearful resistance as trailblazers always do. In fact, even his brother Roy and wife Lily expressed serious concerns about his latest "bright idea". Creating a feature length animated film would cost $500,000; this was more than ten times the cost of the animated shorts they were used to creating. And as work took place on the film, that estimate turned out to be seriously low; the film would eventually cost $1.5 million to create. The buzz in the industry was calling *Snow White* "Disney's Folly" and there were predictions it would sink him into bankruptcy. Keep in mind this was during the Great Depression. This would appear to the fearful as the worst possible time to take a massive new risk.

This bugged Walt, but he sought the advice of positive individuals he'd surrounded himself with. They counseled him to ignore it by saying, *"Let them talk, the more they talk the more attention you're getting, and that's a good thing."* By the end of the creation process, they'd fallen deep into debt with the bank and all eyes were on Walt. Walt's slight fear in the situation could be felt by some of those around him. At one point someone dropped an anonymous note on Walt's desk that said, *"Stick to Shorts"*. Walt was so irritated by this, that for years afterwards when someone made a negative comment to him he'd lash out, *"I'll bet you're the guy who wrote, 'Stick to shorts'!"*

Finally, December 21, 1937, *Snow White and the Seven Dwarfs* was viewed by the public in a glittering premiere at the Carthay Circle Theater in Los Angeles. The big names of Hollywood stepped out of their limousines to attend this pioneering production. Years later, Walt reminisced in delight: *"All the Hollywood brass turned out for my cartoon!"* Inside the theater, the audience laughed at the dwarves and cried when Snow White was found asleep. When the movie ended, the audience stood and cheered!

Snow White was an unheard of success, making $8,000,000! This was an incredible sum based on the fact that ticket prices were just 10 cents for a child and 23 cents for an adult.

Walt was truly elated, and here again is evidence of the heart that was capable of creating so much good. It is my sincere belief Walt did one thing better than anything else...he loved people. He loved to see them laugh and loved to touch their hearts. And he loved to do this by sharing his heart. And what's the secret to love? Faith. Love is always there in the heart of man, but it can't be felt outside the walls of fear. Walt had little fear of himself or others, which allowed him to be his genuine loving self.

Also it's important to remember faith is never based on falsehoods. Walt saw the criticism for what it was; falsehood. The truth he was basing this monumental decision on was that people in the depression needed something uplifting and inspiring more than ever. He believed, even though they didn't, that they DID have the money and would pay to see it. Walt's faith allowed him to see his own inspiration clearly, despite worldly fears. And based on this, he was massively blessed, as was the world.

Living in faith is difficult; just like living in fear is difficult, but for different reasons. Living in faith means being a leader, a pioneer and at times it means being out front and alone. As you see with this eloquent example, Walt's faith brought all of that back to him countless times over. Instead of having to worry about a group of people's criticism and fear, even if that may have included people close to him at times, he won the hearts of the world with his masterpiece, which he was willing to risk everything to create. And the reality is, to him it wasn't risk, it was a calculated plan built on solid natural laws and principles, carefully designed to succeed.

FAITH THROUGH TRAGEDY

New Year's Day 1938 was the golden wedding anniversary of Flora and Elias, and all of the family gathered to celebrate. Walt teased his parents as to whether they were going to "celebrate their marriage" that night. His mother replied, *"We're not a-gonna celebrate."* *"Why not?"* Walt asked. *"We've been celebratin' for fifty years. Gettin' tired of it,"* Flora replied. Walt persisted, *"What about you Dad? Don't you want to make whoopee on your golden wedding anniversary?"* *"Oh, we don't want to go to any extremes a-tall,"* Elias replied. *"Well, I hoped you wouldn't go to any extremes if you're whoopeeing it up."* Walt replied. Flora then interrupted teasing, *"He don't know how to make whoopee."*

Walt's parents were currently living in Portland, Oregon. They still worked fulltime taking care of small apartment houses they owned. When Flora Disney's health broke down, Walt and Roy convinced them it was time to settle down. They bought their parents a comfortable bungalow in North Hollywood, close to Roy's. The senior Disneys had been in the new home less than a month when on November 26, 1938, Flora died of asphyxiation in the night, due to a defective furnace.

I can only imagine the feelings Walt and Roy had to deal with at this point. Here they were finally in a position to take care of their parents and allow them to celebrate their golden years in comfort, and tragedy robs them of this gift. I can't help but think they, would be tempted to blame themselves for the loss. Some of Walt's feelings on this were evident even twenty years later when Walt's secretary casually mentioned his mother's passing. *"I don't want that ever brought up in this office again,"* Walt said sternly, and hurried out of the room.

A situation like this can easily cause a wave of guilt and fear to wash over its victims, and even though we see him struggle, inside, the wolf of faith continues to win as we see Walt move forward in faith. Here again faith tells us, all things are good. Some may call this forgiveness for oneself, but forgiveness denotes a sense of wrong happened that is forgotten. The reality is there was nothing to forgive because what happened wasn't bad. Though it may be natural to see this as bad, nothing that happens is bad, it's all good. It's all for a reason and purpose and our perception of it is everything. Walt dealt with this in a way that did NOT block his heart from the world. Instead he continued to push forward, wielding the power of faith and creation.

A NEW STUDIO, BUILT IN FAITH

Walt continued forward with new feature presentations; *Pinocchio, Fantasia, Dumbo* and *Bambi*. Even though Bambi was meant to be the next film, it ended up in fifth place following *Dumbo*. Again, Walt was pushing past what he'd already learned and ventured into uncharted territory. He found the very foundation of the way they developed the artwork would have to change. He placed his top artists on the job and the studio began to look like a miniature zoo. They brought live animals in to study, as they taught themselves how to capture the beauty of nature in art. Walt instructed the artists not to show him anything until they were personally satisfied with it. When they finally previewed the first completed sections of animation, tears filled Walt's eyes and he said, *"Fellas, this is pure gold."* His faith-powered vision brought another magnificent film to life.

All throughout this growing period for the Disneys, they had spread like wildflowers into a patchwork quilt of buildings across several blocks and pieces of property; some buildings had little to no air conditioning and heating, poor lighting and cramped spaces. Walt's new adventure was to design an entirely new studio from the ground up, or better said, from below the ground up. Walt immersed himself in the new task as he did with everything in life. He dove in head-first and sought to create the very best building he possibly could.

He would create a state-of-the-art building that had a custom designed heating and air conditioning system that also carefully controlled humidity. The studio was a miniature city with its own streets, sewage system, fire hydrants, telephone exchange, and electrical distribution system. Walt even designed special underground tunnels which connected the buildings so workers could easily traverse from one building to another, despite weather conditions. The plan took into consideration the way the sun hit each room, maximizing the light within the building.

Walt's vision was to create a worker's paradise. Everything was designed for the maximum comfort of his co-workers. The buildings wer surrounded by beautiful green lawns where the employees could play baseba badminton and volleyball during lunch hours. They had a modern restaur where they could eat delicious meals at less than the studio's cost. They c also call the snack shop for anything they desired and it would be delive their office. The building included a lounge, soda fountain, sundeck, gym and showers. Walt took this down to the microscopic level by even disr office chairs to see how he could improve them for his artists. He re animation desks to maximize comfort, and reduced wasted time and m furniture, carpets, paint and drapes were all carefully chosen in a harmonious set of pastel colors to provide a restful, quite atmosphere.

Think about what makes a man build a building like that. In business, what typically matters most; the bottom line, right? Where in that decision was Walt most concerned about the bottom line? Intitally it looks like he was foolish. How much money was wasted in frill, fashion, comfort and fun? You could easily say, A LOT. So why did he do it? Was he foolish? And if he was, how did he make foolish, wasteful business decisions, yet still be so successful?

Here's where faith builds upon a much higher law than what we initially see. Walt consciously or unconsciously built upon a higher law which says when you treat people with the best, you'll get the best. Individuals who view things fearfully would say investing that much money was a waste because people won't appreciate it. They'll abuse it. This actually comes from a fear that if I put my best out there, it will be trampled, and the end result is I'll be left hurt by the people I gave my best to.

Walt didn't have this fear. He simply went with his heart and his heart said, "Build the biggest, best, most amazing place you can because that's what you WANT to do, and that's who you are." Again he set a standard for everyone in the business world that may be misunderstood, but was without question, successful.

Previous to this time Elias watched his sons build their business but was constantly hounding them to be careful with their money, to ALWAYS save for a rainy day (which was fear talk for, "always plan on eventual failure or for bad things to happen"). At times he'd complain to his wife, *"Those boys are always borrowing money; they're reckless."*

We can see easily into Elias's fears through his overly powerful sense of thrift. Speaking of which, Walt stated, *"The funny thing is, I didn't inherit any of that thrift, none of it."* Of course my translation of that is: I didn't inherit any of that fear. Yeah, Walt! We most certainly wouldn't know Disney today had he.

Walt and Roy asked their father to supervise the carpentry on the new building, hoping it would help take his mind of the recent loss of his spouse. One day, Walt noticed his father, instead of being excited with all that was going on, becoming more and more concerned. As they walked through the building currently under construction, Elias asked, *"So what can this building be used for?"* Walt wasn't sure what he meant at first, thinking, you know what it's going to be used for...it's our new studio. Then it hit him, he knew what his father was wondering and where the source of concern was. His father was asking "What an this building be used for IF you fail?"

"Walter, how on earth are you going to support this big place with those

*cartoons of yours?—Aren't you **afraid** of you'll go broke?"* Elias asked.

Here again is a glimpse into the hearts of two men and what's fueling the creation of the world around them. We see what's going on in Elias's heart. And it's completely natural...he's scared. But what's most important is to recognize what that fear is doing. Notice how he wants to run in the opposite direction of his son, who's created more in a few years than he's done in his entire life! Despite the evidence and proof of success, his illogical fear drives him the other direction.

Now knowing fear and faith are both contagious energies, what normally happens to a child when their parents fear for them? It's not pretty. Imagine your child doing something that is one of the greatest challenges of their life. Picture them in the midst of overcoming one of their greatest fears. They're walking a tight rope hundreds of feet off the ground. What's going on in their head? Naturally, they're fighting against some serious natural fears.

They're sweating...they know what COULD happen; they know the "risk". And then picture the parent below, staring up in horror and screaming the words, "OH NO! STOP! STOP IT RIGHT NOW! YOU'RE GONNA FALL! YOU'RE GONNA DIE!"

Normally the child seeing the parent as completely wise and most of all truthful then accepts the fear to be truth and falls. HOWEVER, look at Walt. The way he responds, is as though he glances at his father, rolls his eyes and thinks, Oh look, it's the wind beneath my wings.

So here's what he does, as soon as he realizes this is just his father's fears he quickly responds, *"Well, if I do fail, Dad, I can get out easy. You notice how this place is built, with rooms along long corridors? If I go broke with my cartoons, I can always sell it for a hospital."*

What's so funny is Elias was greatly relieved by this explanation from then on. Elias's fears needed a solution to the monster he believed to be real. He was already planning on his son's failure, and as long as there was a plan for how to deal with that failure, he was good. Elias replied to Walt's explanation, *"Oh I see, this would make a perfect hospital."* Walt gave his father a tour of the res of the facility, speaking of it as if it were going to be a hospital!

Notice how Elias obviously had the faith for someone else to successful in that building. Which means he saw "other" people as succes just not himself, which unfortunately also meant, not his son either.

Here we have a perfect display of faith and fear. Walt wouldn't his father's fear, evidenced in that he didn't react with negative energy. accepted some of his father's fear, he'd have responded back in f defensiveness and anger. Instead, he allowed his father to be scared   c through his own faith that even that was okay. It is fear that tells us we need to change, or stop other fearful people. This leads to energy wasted in negativity. Instead, he stayed on his positive path of creation, unphased by his father's fear.

It seemed this was his destiny; to dodge the fears of everyone around him. One day in 1940, Roy asked Walt to come to his office. *"Sit down, kid"* Roy began, shutting the door behind Walt. Roy, taking his place behind his desk, said, *"This is serious. I've got to talk to you."* Roy began the conversation with a healthy dose of fear.

"What's the matter?" Walt asked. Roy outlined the current financial status of their business. How the profits from *Snow White* had been eaten up by the costs of *Pinocchio, Fantasia* and *Bambi*; how the War was seriously impacting sales overseas; how the company now had a thousand employees in a brand-new studio that cost them $3,000,000. *"And now, Walt, we are in debt to the bank for four and half million dollars!"*

What's the one thing that spreads fear so easily? It's the fact that when someone's afraid, they seek comfort in others validating that fear. They need others, especially those close to them to be afraid with them. Roy looked at Walt, expecting the same negative energy to be reflected back to him. If you take a second to think about it, if that were me, I'd probably be pretty open to accepting that fear. I mean, if he thought twice about what his Dad feared, he'd have to tell himself, "Oh crap, here it is, Dad was right I have failed, good thing I've got the hospital back up plan."

But Roy instead of seeing the fear he expected to shroud his younger brother's face, watched as a grin began to grow...and erupt into a fit of laughter. *"What the hell are you laughing at?!"* Roy demanded. Between fits of laughter Walt replied, *"I was just thinking back...Do you remember when we couldn't borrow a thousand dollars?"*

Instead of Roy injecting Walt with fear, Walt overwhelmed Roy with faith and Roy began to laugh as well. *"Yeah, remember how hard it was to get that first twenty-thousand-dollar credit?"* Roy recalled. They laughed back and forth at how they used to plead for loans just to meet the weekly payroll. *"And now we owe four and a half million dollars! I think that's pretty damn good"* Walt laughed.

Then we see Walt's faith come full circle because he first laughs in the face of fear, but he doesn't ignore the issue. Again, it's fear that causes true paralysis, and it would be fear, if anything, that would cause Walt to ignore the facts. Instead he simply deals with the issue in faith by asking his brother, *"What are we going to do?"*

Together they came up with a plan to issue stock. Up to this point, they owned 100% of the company, and now to get on more stable financial ground, they sold $3.5 million worth of stock.

THRIVING IN SPITE OF FEAR

Walt continued to deal with obstacles by finding the way around them. In May 1941, Walt was shocked to find a picket line outside the Disney Studios gate. One of his artists shouted over the loud speaker, *"There he is--the man who believes in brotherhood for everybody but himself."*

The strike became a bitter ordeal for Walt. Here the people whom he'd given his heart to were now lashing out at him, making hurtful and false claims against him. Finally, Walt couldn't take the negativity, and he left to shoot a film in South America. We can see into his feelings through a memo he wrote at the time: *"…The lies, the twisted half-truths that were placed in the public prints cannot be easily forgotten. I was called a rat, a yellow-dog employer and an exploiter of labor. They took the salaries of my messenger boys and claimed them to be the salaries of my artists. My plant and methods were compared to a sweatshop, and above all, I was accused of rolling in wealth. That hurt me most, when the fact is that every damned thing I have is tied up in this business…"*

This is probably the one thing Walt fought the most to get over. He had spread his wings and took under him hundreds of individuals. He sought the best for them. Not because he was just trying to be a good person, but because that's who he truly was. He felt their fearful stabs into his exposed heart and it's said his relationship with his employees was never quite the same.

This brings up the point there are times when others will work in fear to such an extent we cannot change the result they get. They're using the creative power of negativity and they'll get the result from it; they have to, it's a natural law. Just as no one could stop Hitler from destroying his own life, no one could stop the fearful employees from discoloring the walls of their beautiful workplace with their own fear.

It was the fear that the company was going on without them, the fear they weren't going to get "enough". They claimed Walt was becoming vastl· wealthy off of their labors. It turned into a fear-fed fight for their own worth; th· resulted in a loss of what they really needed but couldn't see they already had

It stems from false, fearful beliefs about money. A false belief someone who has a lot of money had to do something bad to get it. This then caused Walt's employees to question him, because in their eyes he h· of money, which means he must have been doing something wrong, a· was doing something wrong, then maybe he's somehow taking adv·

them. I'll attack first and make certain I'm not the fool.

The statement "It's too good to be true" comes from a deep-seated fear we aren't deserving of good things, so when something truly good comes to us, we then have to question it and find the evil therein.

What's amazing is the way Walt handled it. First of all, when he couldn't extinguish the fear-fire with his faith, he just left. He didn't stay around to fight; again he went on to do something positive. Then he let go of their fear. He didn't make it his own; he let it be theirs. We see this by the way he responded to a companion who made a negative comment against the strikers. Walt interrupted, *"Now wait a minute, for whatever reason they did what they did, they thought they were right. We've had our differences on a lot of things, but we're going to continue making pictures, and we're going to find a way to work together."*

Positive, positive, positive, Walt, even in this severe trial of betrayal by his closest friends, is still focused on the way AROUND the obstacle. He's still focused on moving forward. Again he dodges negative energy.

Eventually things were worked out. From a typical business perspective; it was done in an out-of-balance favor to the employees. But again, Walt was determined to keep moving forward.

WALT DISNEY AND ADOLPH HITLER

In December 1941, Walt, still in shock from the news of Pearl Harbor, received a phone call. The studio manager told him, *"Walt the studio police just phoned me; the Army is moving in on us."*

The US Army took over the entire Walt Disney Studio, turning the artist studios into sleeping quarters for soldiers, the storage garages were filled with ammunition, and the auditorium was converted into a repair station for trucks and anti-aircraft guns. All employees were fingerprinted and given badges to get in and out of the Disney Studios / US Army base.

Walt could have viewed this as the end, yet again we see him find the good. Immediately, the government began to request war support films, and Walt was glad to oblige. The war itself would seriously affect the income of the Disney Enterprise. However, instead of going under, the organization that was accustom to producing 30,000 feet of film per year previous to the war, skyrocketed to 300,000 feet per year based on war films. Here again was another opportunity for Disney to see something as bad, when in reality; they learned how to increase normal production by ten times!

One particular war propaganda film which Disney Studios created starred Donald Duck and was called *Der Fueher's Face*. The storyline showed Donald having a nightmare in which he dreamed he was working in a German munitions factory. The film helped expose the reality of Hitler's actions, and was translated into all European languages and smuggled into the continent by the underground, infuriating the Nazi High Command.

About the same time Hitler came to power, Mickey Mouse was an idol to German children, much like any other country at the time. I wrote much about Hitler, and his aversion to positive energy. It's amazing to notice how he reacts to Disney's fruits. Once during one of his frantic speeches, he was quoted in the press as saying, *"Why are the blond youth of Germany wearing the emblem of this vile scum, Mickey Mouse? Down with Mickey Mouse! Wear the swastika."* Roy commented, *"And just like that they all quit. Because they had the fear of God on them then."*

It's funny how easily Roy nailed Hitler's power of control, *"because they had the FEAR of God on them."* Think about the power that caused all those children to be drawn to that simple icon. At the time, Mickey pins were a big hit, a simple piece of plastic shaped and painted in the form of a mouse that could be pinned on. Have you ever thought why? Why does that have any value at all? You can't eat it. And technically, except to other children, it would have no value whatsoever. So why were they so drawn to it?

The answer is simple, it's **energy**. All things have an energy source, and those trinkets were of value because the energy they were charged with. It was a piece of Walt's heart. The energy coming from that little icon is one of the strongest forms of positive energy we have in our world today. I can ask you what the Mickey icon stands for, and nearly every person in the world could respond in a similar manner and it would be something positive, except Hitler of course. Conversely, the swastika, a symbol of negative energy, was not espoused by anyone outside the control of fear.

The energies radiated by the Mickey Mouse symbol are: fun, happiness, child-like-excitement, love, being a child, success, motivation, family entertainment, family value, friends, and on and on; all of the responses being descriptions of positive energy, or in other words faith. I mentioned love because at the core, that's really what positive energy is. Walt's view of love was simple yet profound. To his secretary one day he said, *"Hazel, let's face it--love is li⅃ everything else; if you don't have it, you can't give it."* At his core, Walt's stren⅃ was having little, if any, walls blocking the love in his heart.

What's amazing is when you work in positive faithful energy, attr⅃ others is effortless. Walt didn't have to sell a single child on Micke⅃ instinctively knew how it made them feel...good. Kids are for the most ⅃

free, and they are instantly drawn to anything of a positive nature.

Contrastingly, Hitler worked strictly from a place of fear. So to accomplish his designs, he was only able to use the tools of fear. He controlled an entire nation and most of the world using fear. It's easy to picture the night–and–day difference between faith and fear in this situation. Hitler was behind the whole world, snapping a whip, pushing and pushing incessantly, miserably living out his worst fears, while Walt was in front of the whole world, leading effortlessly by simply following his heart, living his dreams.

POST WAR FAITH

By 1945, the war had ended and the Disney organization was changed. Overseas income was nearly non-existent, since funds were held overseas due to post-war economical problems. They were $4,000,000 in debt to the bank again. Roy knew he could do nothing to make Walt dismantle the business in any way in order to cut costs. Walt always saw the solution as we'll just *"Lick'em with product."* It was another way of saying, "No we won't retreat; we'll get even more aggressive." Finally, Roy told the bank to stop beating him up over the debt. If they wanted anything done they'd have to talk to Walt himself.

So Joe Rosenberg, the bank representative, paid a visit to Walt. Joe began doing his best to convey the "seriousness" of the situation to Walt. He used the fact that he had investors they were responsible to, etc. And no matter how friendly they felt towards the Disneys, they MUST protect their investors. *"Are you finished?"* Walt interrupted.

Joe continued, *"No. Roy and I are agreed that you must cut down on your outgo drastically. Your expenses each week are entirely too high in light of the amount of income you are receiving. You've simply got to cut back."* "Is that all?" Walt asked. *"No, let me finish, let me finish."* Rosenburg went on with his lecture, despite Walt's interruptions. Finally, Rosenburg said, *"All right, I'm finished. What have you got to say?"*

Walt looked out the window at the falling rain and simply stated, *"You know, I'm disappointed in you, Joe. I thought you were a different kind of banker. But it turns out you're just a regular god-damned banker. You'll loan a guy an umbrella on a sunshiny day, but when it rains you want it back."*

The faith that kept driving Walt forward eventually pushed Roy well outside his circle of faith. Roy began pulling back on Walt, demanding he not work on any more big productions and that he cut back. Finally after a long debate, Roy snapped, *"Look--you're letting this place drive you to the nuthouse. That's one place I'm not going with you!"* The next morning Walt entered Roy's office emotional and said, *"Isn't it amazing what a horse's ass a fellow can be sometimes?"*

What's unique about this situation is most relationships would have caved under the pressure of fear. Here, these two are talking about failure in the biggest way! Here, they're world renown. From a fearful perspective, you look at this scenario and think; the higher you climb, the further you fall. But yet these two didn't let fear destroy their relationship. The very next morning Walt and Roy remembered what was most important to them, and let go of their fears.

You can see how Walt dealt with the banker's fear tactics. The banker used guilt against Walt, as if he was personally hurting investors. Walt wasn't ignoring these people or trying to hurt them. Faith releases guilt and focuses on solutions. And that's just what he did. Walt began work on the next smash hit, *Cinderella,* which helped to cut their debt by more than half by 1950.

Another great example of how Walt viewed money was in building his own personal railroad. Most of us give up our childhood dreams to the fears of the real world, but not Walt. He kept that child alive within him. Walt had a love of trains, and as an adult, had to have one. He built a one-eighth-scale model of an old Central Pacific Railroad train and built a ½ mile run for the train in his back yard. In one section, Walt wanted the train go underground through a curved tunnel. To this idea his foreman suggested, *"Walt, it'd be a lot cheaper if you built the tunnel straight."* Walt replied, *"Hell, it'd be cheaper not to do this at all!"* Then he gave his secretary, who paid all his bills, strict instructions NOT to tell him how much the tunnel cost to build.

Walt believed money was only good for what you could do with it. Money served him and not the other way around. He always kept his sight set on his visions, dreams, and goals and went over, around, and under any fears that threatened to stop him.

HIS GREATEST VISION

In the early 1950s, Walt had diversified, seeking new challenges. The Disney organization was now producing all types of entertainment media. They produced films about nature, such as the *Living Desert,* which was the first of it' kind, starting an entirely new genre of film entertainment. They produc' fictional films such as *20,000 Leagues Under the Sea* and new and exci' animated films such as *Lady and the Tramp.*

At this time, something else was brewing in Walt's mind. Walt h' beautiful daughters, Sharon and Diane, who were the light of his life. It any spare time he had was spent with them. Many times he'd bring them to the office on the weekends where they'd ride bikes and play while he caught up on things. He also loved taking them to all sorts of entertainment venues, such as fairs, carnivals, zoos, circuses and national parks. Everywhere they went around the world, Walt would make it a point to visit any entertainment possible.

Because of what this time with his girls meant to him, he determined his next adventure would be in building his own amusement park. He'd seen them all and most were not even close to what he felt they should be. He was critical of how dirty and run-down most amusement parks were. He knew the right way to do it and was determined to do so. He knew what those times with his daughters meant to him and knew what it would mean to the world if it was done right.

When Walt approached Roy with the idea, poor Roy could do nothing more than seriously oppose the idea. From Roy's perspective they were finally getting to a place of financial security and this was the wildest of any of Walt's ideas so far. I'm sure Roy was probably ready to jump off the Walter-Coaster by this point.

Walt again simply went around the obstacle; he started his own company, Walt Disney, Inc. under which he began the process of starting his vision he now called *Disneyland*. He began borrowing against his own life insurance policy until he'd maxed it out at $100,000 in debt.

One day, Roy received a call from a banker friend who said Walt had visited him and told him about his idea for Disneyland. The banker said it was a wonderful idea. Roy questioned the banker about his younger brother, *"Did Walt try to borrow money from you?"* The banker replied, *"Yes, he did. And you know what? I loaned it to him!"*

By 1953, money was running out, and Walt knew he had to find another source of funding. The idea came to him while he lay sleepless in bed, *"Television!"* Walt went straight to Roy the next morning to propose how they'd pay for the park, they'd use television. Not only would television give them a source of income, but it would also be the way they'd advertise the park. This became the start of the hit television series *The Wonderful World of Disney*. Now that he could see the answer, Roy was finally sold on the idea, but they still had board members to convince.

Walt went before the board to present his vision. Conservative board members complained that they were not in the amusement-park business, to which Walt replied that the company WAS in the entertainment business. Walt then went on to convey his absolute faith in himself and his vision. He admitted it would be hard for them to envision it the way he could, but he'd been around the world and he knew just about everything there was to know about what he wanted to do.

He then said, *"I don't want this company to stand still. We have prospered before because we have taken chances and tried new things. Disneyland will prosper because it's unique, there's nothing like it in the entire world. I know because I've looked. A new concept in entertainment, and I think... I KNOW...it can be a success."* Walt's amazing energy filled the room, his eyes filled with testimonial tears of his faith. The board members couldn't deny the power and were persuaded.

Walt's amazing power of faith began to create the crowning achievement of his life. Walt's faith helped him see all men as good, and thus his goal was to build something worthy of these "good" people. When he looked at any attraction, his deciding factor was not what it cost or whether he personally liked it, it was whether or not "the people" would like it. If he felt it passed, he'd say, *"I think they'll go for this"* or *"They're going to eat this up."* If he didn't feel the attraction was up to this standard he'd say, *"That's not good enough for them"* or *"They'll expect something better."*

l "them" short. Walt was once ney on beautiful flowers, shrubs people would just trample and him that attractions might be *'t worry about it. Just make them they all have it; all you have to do is*

ry about it. Don't be AFRAID of e; this is his fuel of passion, his e. Notice this in contrast to Hitler 1other.

A DREAM

13, 1955, Walt would invite a special isneyland. That evening their guests to a tour of his latest creation. He led dock of the Mark Twain paddle boat. Its creating a jubilant environment. Waite boat pulled away from the dock, whi

s of envisioning had finally come to l'

most of all, he was finally able to share this special vision with the people he loved. He visited with his guests until the boat came to rest where the group was moved to the Golden Horseshoe for dinner. Their entertainment was performed by the high-kicking chorus girls and stand-up comic Wally Boag. Walt had gone up into the balcony and leaned over the stage when people started noticing him.

As people began to cheer, Walt became encouraged, and like a little boy began to climb over the balcony down to the stage. At one point, things got a little scary, but he finally made it safely on stage. The crowd cheered, and Walt just stood there beaming. Everyone started chanting, *"Speech! Speech!"* but Walt didn't say a thing, he just stood there smiling. Then everyone started chanting for Lily. *"We want Lily!"* Finally Lily went on stage dragging daughter Sharon with her. The crowd applauded the family and still no word from Walt who continued to stand and grin from ear to ear.

That night on the car ride home, Walt had a map of Disneyland rolled up. He blew it as if it were a trumpet in Sharon's ear; and before long she turned around to see her father, curled up in the back seat, arms around his rolled up map, sound asleep like a little boy worn out from his playing.

A MAN OF REAL POWER

I'm not sure if my words can convey the feelings I have for this situation, but I am touched to my core by the child-like, innocent faith of this sweet man. He truly was the boy who refused to grow up, or in my words, the boy who refused to live in a world of fear. He chose to see the world through the rose-colored glasses of faith and then saw that world become his reality. Standing on stage, I know there was no need for words. Walt had already said everything his heart had to say by his actions. His guests were surrounded by the beliefs of his heart in physical reality; a place of fun, laughter, joy and most of all, love. What else was there to say?

What he got most from that singular experience was to bask in the joy of his friends. The road Walt traveled was lonely at times. It was just him upfront, leading everyone else. At the end of the road, when everyone reached the destination with Walt, he finally was able to celebrate with them in his ultimate goal to share the joy and beauty he felt inside with everyone around him.

The next morning Walt bounded out of the house at 7:30, back to Disneyland again for the grand opening. I was fortunate to get a copy of the DVD, *Walt – The Man Behind the Myth*. It's a beautiful production about his life. It contains a section showing the live footage of Walt cutting the ribbon on the opening day of *Disneyland*. His daughter Diane opens the scene saying, *"You could see the lump in Dad's throat and the tears in his eyes."* Then it shows Walt standing in front of the red ribbon at the entrance, giving the following dedication:

"To all who come to this happy place, welcome. Disneyland is your land. Herein lives fond memories of the past and here youth may savor the challenge and promise of the future. Disneyland is dedicated to the ideals, the dreams and facts that have created America, with the hope that it will be a source of joy and inspiration to all the world. Thank you."

As I watched, I was overwhelmed. Never have I felt words spoken with more honesty and sincerity in my life. I was trying to write down the words, but I was crying at the same time and couldn't see what I was writing. So I had to keep rewinding and replaying it. I was so sincerely touched by the love and power of this man, it blew me away. He's long since been gone from this earth, yet his love, faith and vision impacted me with such real power.

That opening day, according to news reports, was a disaster. All kinds of things went wrong, yet characteristically Walt didn't dwell on it. Despite the mishaps of opening day, *Disneyland* went on to exceed even Walt's expectations. Today it is the standard of amusement and entertainment for the entire world. *Disneyland* alone insured once and for all Disney's financial security. The one last idea Roy feared could mean their ultimate financial ruin, would become their ultimate savior. Later, it would be Roy that carried on Walt's dream to create *Disney World* and *Epcot*.

I've given a snapshot of events in Walt's life that demonstrated how he worked, or more importantly how he believed. This of course is just the tip of the iceberg and I could go on and on, but most importantly I feel I've communicated the powerful truth the fueled him.

LEAVING A LEGACY

December 1966, Walt Disney passed away. His death rocked the world. Newspapers around the globe wrote of the news. A Paris newspaper stated, *"All the children in the world are in mourning. And we have never felt so close to them."* Another in Holland called Walt Disney a king who *"reigned for several decades over the fantasy of children in all the world."* Dwight D, Eisenhower commented, *"His appeal and influence were universal. Not restricted to this land alone--for he touched common chord in all humanity. We shall not soon see his like again."*

From the White House, President Lyndon B. Johnson wrote to Lilly *a sad day for America and the world when a beloved artist leaves us. Millions of us lived a brighter and happier life by the light of your husband's talents. We mourn him and miss him with you. The magic of Walt Disney was larger than life, and the treasures he left will endure to entertain and enlighten worlds to come."*

Eric Sevareid on the CBS Evening News seemed to express the feelings of people around the world with his words: *"It would take more time than anybody has around the daily new shops to think of the right thing to say about Walt Disney. He was an original; not just an American original, but an original, period. He was a happy accident; one of the happiest this century has experienced; and judging by the way it's been behaving in spite of all Disney tried to tell it about laughter, love, children, puppies and sunrises, the century hardly deserved him. He probably did more to heal or at least to soothe troubled human spirits than all the psychiatrists in the world. There can't be many adults in the allegedly civilized parts of the globe who did not inhabit Disney's mind and imagination at least for a few hours and felt better for the visitation..."*

I have to add my own personal interpretation of what the world struggled to put into words about this amazing man.

At a very special time in the history of this world, at a time when the world would experience one of the greatest floods of fear. Being drowned in all the negative fruits of fear… war, death, violence, and depression, the world was given a very special light. A light that brought balance, a light that if men choose to look to, would confirm their free agency to choose faith and disregard fear, to find hope and peace midst the storm. The legacy he left behind is one that's blessed all humanity. Walt Disney spoke a language every person in this world understood: hope and love.

HIS SECRET TO SUCCESS

I've read several individual's attempts to decode Disney's success in a digestible form. Looking at Disney without the clarity of faith leaves one scratching their head for understanding because here are the facts: Walt wasn't educated by the world's standards. He dropped out after the 9th grade, refusing to spend one more day in school. His parents were not in any special position to give him a "leg-up" in the world. He wasn't even the best artist! Most people simply walk away in confusion chalking it up to him being a genius. Yet again, it wasn't because he somehow had some super abnormal knowledge or experience in building a business. In fact, you could easily argue he ran his business in the red throughout the majority of his career.

So what was "it"? What did he have that seems so elusive to the average individual? The answer is simple… pure faith. The greatest part is Walt didn't need success to make him happy. In fact it never works that way because success is a choice, a belief, a perspective. Walt chose to be happy first, and that's what brought the fruits of happiness or success. Once you tell the universe you are happy, it will respond with all of the "symptoms" of happiness. You have to have the disease before you can have the symptoms.

He was true to himself, which means he recognized the truth within himself. The truth that he was inherently good, and so were his fellowmen. With this foundational belief, what is there to fear?

One day I had a friend ask me in frustration, why are you so successful? I'm just as talented and smart as you are. Why are you successful and I'm not? I laughed to him later about the conversation because at the time I was financially bankrupt and in the process of losing much of what I've worked to gain. What he saw in me at the time though wasn't fear of what I was going through. What he saw was the faith of where I was going to. After this I began to tell people I came into this discussion with: People wrongly suspect that I am happy because I am successful. However the opposite is the case. I am successful because I am happy. Happiness always has been and always will be the only true measure of success.

THE DIFFERENCE

Here's where we define the difference between Hitler and Disney. While one man in fear created weapons to destroy, another man in faith created entertainment design to give hope. While the one created concentration camps to enslave, the other made amusement parks to set the child within us free. While one set out to control the hearts of men with fear, the other sought to fill the hearts of men with love.

While one fought with all his might to force others down a road of hopelessness, the other led effortlessly his fellow man to follow their dreams. While one fought to extinguish the bad he feared in his enemies, the other sought to inspire the good he saw in his fellow man.

It left us with a simple choice as to what were we going to hail; be it the light or the darkness, faith or fear? No I don't think we can say that "good" had left us during that period. It was always there should we choose to see it. It always is.

The greatest miracle is that though this sweet man no longer walks th' mortal path; the power of his faith continues to work in the hearts of men, i' never-ending circle of creative power. We'll never lose Walt Disney excep' fearful denial of what he chose to see as real.

In the New Testament, the book of Mathew 18:3 reads, *"...I say unto you, Except ye be converted, and become as little children, ye shall not enter into the kingdom of heaven."* What was it that Walt so clearly understood about this illusive principle? Walt clearly sought to live the vow of a character he brought to life, *Peter Pan*, to never grow up. But what is it that is so powerful about this principle? Was it a silly refusal to take responsibility in life? Was it an ignorant denial of reality?

Think about it, what is the defining characteristic that differentiates children from adults? You know what I'm going to say, so go ahead and say it with me. Faith. Isn't the purest form of faith stated as child-like faith? Walt's intention wasn't a refusal to get older or to somehow stop physical growth or aging. Walt's belief in not growing up was a belief in not losing his child-like faithful view of this amazing wonderful world. He refused to view the world as something to be afraid of, unlike most of us as adults. Most of all, he refused to become afraid of himself, of his heart. He trusted it to the end. And by so doing, he gives permission to the whole world to do the same. Right now, no matter the situation or circumstance, he gives us permission to love ourselves, and to love and trust that sweet faithful child within us.

CHAPTER 12

TM

THE CONCLUSION

Okay, now here's where the rubber meets the road. I don't think many individuals will have much difficulty accepting that Walt Disney was a good man. However, it's vital I make this point as clearly as possible. The intention of this analysis of these two men was not to paint the typical black-and-white picture of good and bad. Again, this is our natural tendency, and it's crucial I clarify there is no such thing as "bad", especially when we are considering people. Remember that it is this very fearful belief that was one of the core beliefs that fueled Hitler. And, the opposite of this belief is exactly what fueled Disney. So let's take Disney's quote, "… *appeal to the best side of people. They ALL have it; all you have to do is bring it out.*"

They all have it! He's stating a powerful belief of faith that all mankind have good in them, you just have to bring it out. And I'm going to add my belief to further clarify, that ALL men ARE good. Not just a part of them, which could leave room for a part of them to be evil as well. Every part of them is good. The only negative that comes from man is due to fear, NOT due to inherent evil.

Disney chose what he would focus on, which was that good he believed to exist in people. Hitler chose to focus on the bad he believed to exist in people. Where we begin to truly get Disney's powerful secret to happiness and success is when we choose to no longer see people as either good people doing good things or evil people doing evil things. But start to see all people as either one of two types: good and faithful people that see things positively, or good but fear

---

153

people that see things negatively.

Again, if we go back to the fear that Hitler was somehow evil, and we try to discern what it was that made him evil, we'll come out confused and frustrated. For example, if we try to analyze the things that made these men different, we find they are more alarmingly alike than we'd have even guessed.

THE COMPARISON

Both men were raised in very similar circumstances. Both had loving mothers, and both lost their mothers in difficult ways. Coincidentally even in name these mothers were similar, Flora and Klara. However, if either should have had the tendency to view their mother's death more negatively, it should have actually been Walt who could have easily blamed himself for the loss.

Both had very similar, fearful fathers. Remember they didn't have bad fathers, but fathers who struggled with fear. It's very clear both fathers loved their sons. I was amazed when I found they even shared the same name. Alois translated from German to English is Elias! Both boys felt a desire to become artists, and both dealt with their father's rejection of it. Both struggled to become artists as their faith was tried. Both saw some success in their talent, yet both eventually would not generate their income through it.

Both men would eventually become world renowned in a way few men in history ever have been or ever will be. Their names would be known in every household, in every corner of the world. Both were raised in a Christian religion, yet neither would be regular, formal church attendees as adults. Both were absolute patriots to their countries and played roles in both World Wars. Both suffered poverty. Both knew financial success. Both had a very similar minimal education, dropping out of school around the age of 16; neither obtaining a high school diploma. Ironically Walt was even accused of being a racist, anti-Semitic, and communistic.

It's even interesting to me that I found pictures of Walt in the late 1930s which show him with just a little bit of the ends of his moustache trimmed off. Not to the extent of Hitler's, but how ironic he would even have some slightly similar physical appearances.

Now if you're thinking to yourself, so what, big deal? These similarities mean nothing, then you're absolutely right. They don't mean anything and that's my point. None of these things determined whether or not these men were good or evil. We have to throw out education, upbringing, financial status, religion, race, etc. in the comparison. In this situation, none of these things could have been a defining factor in these individuals personal makeup. These were all outside things. Yet here is where the similarities end.

One simple fact shows the clearest difference between these two men...pictures. If you Google images of Hitler and Disney you'll instantly notice the glaring difference. In nearly every picture taken of Disney he is happy. In nearly every picture of Hitler he is unhappy.

Of course the foundational difference that made ALL the difference was within their belief. One chose to live in a dark world he saw through the eyes of fear, the other chose to live in a beautiful world he saw through the eyes of faith.

CHAPTER 13

™

LIVE FEAR-LESS

It's been my privilege to share this journey with you. Due to this new perspective, my life has changed more in the last three years than I ever could have imagined. The greatest part is knowing we've only scraped the surface. I'm excited to write about these changes. This is just the first of a new flow of information. This book is simply an introduction to the topic. Future books will follow with more information and tools to give greater clarity.

Fear vs. Faith is a culture, a language that's above race, religion and creed. It's designed to bring down walls and give us the tools to move forward in faith. I hope that sharing my heart with you has brought you a measure of peace and hope.

The next question is where do we go from here? The answer is it's up to you. You are the creator of your world.

Start by asking yourself the following questions:

What, right now, do I feel the inspiration to do?
What fears stand in my way?
Am I moving forward in my life or just treading water?
How is fear affecting my relationships with others?
How do I view my past, as failure or progression?
What do I fear the most?

Who do I fear?

Most of all, how do I view myself?

I have to close with the simple, words of the Disney classic, *When You Wish Upon a Star* introduced in *Pinocchio*, the powerful message of which is a boy who desperately wanted to be "real". It all came true based on his faith. As you read, think of the man who brought these words to life through his amazing faith.

When you wish upon a star
Makes no difference who you are
Anything your heart desires
Will come to you

If your heart is in your dream
No request is too extreme
When you wish upon a star
As dreamers do

Fate is kind
She brings to those who love
The sweet fulfillment of
Their secret longing

Like a bolt out of the blue
Fate steps in and sees you through
When you wish upon a star
Your dreams come true

If you look closely all of the principles of faith are right there! It's time to accept this amazing power in our lives. It's time to be happy. It's time to dream!

For more information go to: www.Live-Fearless.com

RECOGNITION

I have to take time to recognize the amazingly faithful people in my life that made this a reality.

MY SWEET WIFE: Her pure faith-filled love for me has truly saved my life and filled me up to overflowing. I love you.

SUE KINKEAD: Other-mother of faith; before her email, my book was something I just talked about. She wrote me one day, telling me I needed to start it now! Since then she has been my number one reader and supporter. Her tearful testimonies that what I was doing was good kept me going when fear threatened to stop me. Thank you Sue, I love you.

LANCE RICH: Older brother; always unconditional faith in me. Where my father's faith ended, Lance's began. Thank you for being true to yourself and giving me the permission to do so as well. I love you.

GAVIN RICH: Younger brother; though we have traveled far from where we were belief-wise, you've always been right there with me. I love you.

MICHAEL J. WORLTON: Editor, brother-in-law, and wonderful friend; Michael took the challenge of editing the book. His insight and faith have greatly enhanced and supported this message. Thank you, my brother-in-faith. I love you.

BRANDON WIESNER: Brother-in-law, partner and long-time friend; he's always been there, someone who's just as crazy as I am about living dreams. It was his love for Walt Disney and his recommendation that caused me to read it. Thank you for all of your faith and support. You're an amazing partner! I love you.

TODD SMITH: Brother-in-law, successful entrepreneur and powerful friend; it was Todd that has recommended life-changing books that were keys to finding answers to my own conflicting foundation beliefs. Todd has been one individual who lived his life fearlessly. He is an amazing example to me of its power. He has been another pillar of strength for me. One day amidst a dark, fear-filled time I sat at my desk grasping for hope. I began searching for the light, something to deny the darkness that felt so real around me. Just then a text appeared on my phone. It was from Todd and read, *"I have a strong feeling you need to get your book edited and to the masses now…ASAP"*. It may seem like a small thing but it was the light that split the darkness for me that day. Thank you for following your heart Todd. I love you.

KATY REES: Sister-in-law, and first willing-editor. When I started the book I didn't know what I was doing. Katy volunteered to help me edit it. She was a great support and positive source of energy when the book was in its infant stages. Thank you for your sweet faith and support. I love you.

BIBLIOGRAPHY

Type	Author	Title	Publisher	Date
DVD	History Channel	The Brain	A & E Television Networks	2008
Book	Adolph Hitler	Mein Kampf	Mariner Books	9/15/98
Book	Bob Thomas	Walt Disney: An American Original	Disney Editions	4/15/94
Book	Bob Thomas	Building a Company: Roy O. Disney and the Creation of an Entertainment Empire	Disney Editions	7/8/98
Article	Elie Weisel	Adolph Hitler	Time Magazine	4/13/98
Book	Dr. Wayne Dyer	The Power of Intention	Hay House	2/23/04

All Scriptural References taken from the Bible, King James Version.